THE *Truth* ABOUT THE *Lie I Live*

ALSO *by* C. NaTASHA RICHBURG

Life: What's Up with Yours?

Who's Renting Space in Your Head?

Every Story Has Two Sides

www.theCNRMinistries.com

C. NaTasha Richburg

THE *Truth* ABOUT THE *Lie I Live*

THE TRUTH ABOUT THE LIE I LIVE

PERMISSION TO QUOTE:

"In every cloud, there is a silver lining."
Working through the cloud strengthens your ability
to grab the lining and hold on.

Contents

Foreword

*W*HAT A MOVING AND POWERFUL message to inspire and speak power and truth to those of us (especially our youth) who have or continue to live behind a mask of pain. The mask has many names — shame, fear, physical abuse, mental abuse, promiscuity, porn addiction, sexual assault, self doubt, not feeling good enough or worthy enough – all of which are manifested in so many destructive ways that cut us off from receiving God's love and healing power.

With this book, Mrs. NaTasha Richburg's prophetic voice speaks in the vernacular of the young with a rawness and honesty that is designed to reach them where they are. The characters are fictional but the demons that many of them struggle with are common place but not necessarily made transparent nor dealt with openly; hence the characters wear their masks. And, they struggle needlessly until they surrender to the will of God.

The most powerful message in this woven tapestry of rich and colorful characters is that "GOD is still in charge." The God of Abraham and the God of "the Women at the Tomb" is the same God whose blood still heals and restores us to the abundant life that He promised.

The Truth About the Lie I Live provides a roadmap to victory. The subtext is quite simple: "Let Go and Let God." As you read further, you will identify a recurring message that God can make all things right no matter how hopeless or wrong the situation may seem.

There is no hiding place from God because He knows all and sees all. In Psalm 32:7, we read "You are my hiding place; you will protect me from trouble and surround me with songs of deliverance." We learn that it is only when we surrender to His word and will that God brings grace and healing to any situation.

This roadmap is interspersed with scriptural readings, rhythmic verses for reflection, and thought provoking questions to challenge our thinking and to begin a dialogue of forgiveness and healing. In Isaiah 41:13, He says, "For I am the Lord, your God, who takes hold of your right hand and says to you, do not fear; I will help you." This book is a call to a personal invitation to seek God and to receive his love, whatever your circumstance, no matter which mask you are wearing.

For those of us who are still wearing a mask, let this powerful message challenge us to experience the pain and vulnerability of being stripped bare in honesty and truth before God our Father so that we may be healed. Let's seek His guidance through prayer, and be open to receive Him through his many messengers; i.e., our ministers, family members, friends or professionals.

Mrs. Richburg invites us to, "Trust in the Lord with all your heart; and don't lean on your own understanding. In all things acknowledge Him, and He shall direct your way" (Proverbs 3:5, 6). God is ready to do what we cannot do by ourselves. This is your personal invitation. Don't forget to RSVP!

Brenda J. Sykes

"To whom much is given, much is expected" (Luke 12:48). Instilled by her mother at a very early age, Brenda Joyce Sykes continues to be guided by this credo. Married to Napoleon for 38 years, Brenda is the mother of three extraordinary adults who are a constant source of pride. After retiring from the federal government as a senior executive with 33 years of public service, Brenda remains excited and lives in anticipation of the new doors that God continues to open and the wonderful opportunities that await her.

Introduction

$\mathcal{T}$HERE ARE EXPERIENCES IN LIFE that shape our approach for obtaining a deeper understanding of life's circumstances. Negative circumstances such as sexual abuse, child abuse, emotional abuse and neglect, may scare us into a shell that poses as a defense mechanism to mask the pain. Embodied in the shell is an opportunity to mature our dreams, that when released into the world, serve as a chance to regain balance. As long as we continue to try to maneuver our way out of our shells, our muscles will pulsate with repetitious energy so that we emerge stronger, wiser, and ready to explode into our destiny.

Love is an expression that motivates us into action. Love tells us the truth so that we will become better. Love holds us tight in our mother's womb. Love lets us run fast, jump, and scrape our knees. God is Love and Love is God. Love language expressed to our liking warms our souls. When we trust love to heal, we use it to uncover the public mask to reveal truth about who we really are. Some of us are who the world see. For others, the public face masks the lie we live.

Follow the stories of Angel, Brock, Free Will, Rome, Kasha, and Alex as they effectively manage the trials and tribulations of life while seeking the chance to remove the mask that uncovers an understanding of their love language that celebrates who they really are. Physical, sexual, emotional, drug abuse and neglect reside behind the mask of their seemingly normal lives. This secret, once released into the blossom of God, motivates them to face the chance to overcome the odds presented to them or fall prey to deviant behavior.

For each character in the book, *God is the answer*—not just a saying. God is the focal point used to handle each of them, as the masks are removed one person at a time. *The Truth About the Lie I Live* embraces the importance of how truth in God will crack the shells that bind our existence. It is through God's love that wounds are open to the possibility to receive love from others.

CHAPTER ONE

Songs of Freedom

"...He entered a house and did not want anyone to know it; yet he could not keep his presence secret."

Mark 7:24 (NIV)

Angel Johnson

THE VERY LIKABLE ANGEL JOHNSON lived vicariously through the experiences of others. Everyone's friend at the ripe old age of fifteen, she had the honor of being the person that everyone loved to confide in because she could hold a secret. Angel held her own secret—she could sing like a bird. Her voice was held in the place of privacy where onlookers could not view. Careful to conceal her talent, it was her most favorite obsession in the world to sing at the top of her lungs in the bathroom and in an empty house. God had given Angel the ability to hit the high notes like Mariah Carey with the soulfulness of Mary J. Blige.

Angel loved the Lord and wanted to please Him by singing the tunes of the gospel greats. Soulful tunes graced her vocal cords. A familiar cool breeze cleansed the worries of failure. Success chilled her skin. The selection for the day encapsulated her mood. The newer artists like Mary Mary, Yolanda Adams, CeCe Winans and more, were the model of what it is like to sing from the depth of your spirit. Angel allowed the Holy Spirit to move through her in the form of a new dance every week. Seasoned artists like Shirley Caesar and Dorothy Norwood demonstrated soul-stirring movement that inspired healing passion to reveal itself through Angel. When the Spirit rested heavily on Angel, she would bend down as she leaned to the left, symbolizing a tugging at her heart. The grabbing and tugging mixed the melody prior to it belting out in the form of a song. Her favorite artist is herself, Angel Johnson, obsessed to sing out loud, relieving all pent up emotions, passion, and praise.

The opening passage of Angel's diary written on her fifteenth birthday reads: *Staring into the eyes of the first man I loved are the eyes of my father set squarely in the center of my face as I look into the mirror. I look exactly like him. The almond brown color of my skin matches his skin color exactly. The texture of my hair, in which my mother is most graceful, curls exactly like his. My curls brush out nicely with a little water on the dampened hair brush dipped in light hair conditioner.*

I remember his hugs and the bristles on his face that scratched my cheeks when he kissed me. The bristles were his 5:00 shadow, when coupled with the smell of nice after shave lotion, encouraged me to run playfully from my father whenever he came around. He did not come around much in the early days. I loved who he was in my life.

My father was the one that represented fun—the good times. He was not the one to tell me when to go to bed or wake me up in the morning. He was the man who lived life on his own terms, even if it meant I would plop into the chair at the front door for many hours waiting for him to arrive, only for him not to show up again—and again—and again.

I would recall in my mind his promise to come at 2:00 only to arrive at 5:30 wondering why I was not ready. I was always happy to see him no matter the time he arrived, while at the same time being angry for anticipating that maybe he would not come again. Maybe that is why I cannot take riding roller coasters, with all the ups and downs, such as my father going and coming without the benefit of an announcement. My stomach continued dropping out to the bottom when the dip of his unreliability was steeper than I anticipated. The dip just never felt good to me because the drop in my stomach was always followed by a ride to the next peak. When Daddy arrived it was a peak.

My father was the huggy one. My mother was not. So when he did hug me, it felt a little uncomfortable because I was not used to being hugged and kissed. It was his smile, the smell of fresh fried scallops and Triple Decker sandwiches that said, "I was loved and cherished; I was special. I was Daddy's little girl."

At two years old, I lost the only man in my life because he could not get along with my mother. My man. My father. My daddy was gone. Around my heart now is a shield that protects me from ever having the feeling of loss again. God predestined the bond I had with my daddy. In those days, I trusted he would be in place even if he arrived a little late. I just needed to give him something to be proud of.

I look in the mirror and realize I am a combination of both my parents' ancestry, and more importantly, I am one of God's children. I see my father's eyes. I feel rage because over the years I became one of his "after thoughts." After he finished with his new wife, step children, his friends, his business, his good government job, then he would think about me. After he had one moment to himself and everything in his life was in place, then maybe he thought about me. His "after thought" attention was my father's attempt to get a pat on the back for doing right by me.

I see his eyes in the mirror, though he is gone home to be with the Lord. I see his eyes; I need to feel good about him so I can feel good about me. When I am able to look into the eyes of that special man and not feel pain, I will know deliverance has arrived for me.

Five Years Later

AT JEREMIAH'S CALL CAFÉ, TWENTY-YEAR-OLD Angel recalled her friend, Free Will, the Christian poet who was the headliner for the evening—the situation that changed her life. *One Saturday morning I waited patiently for all in the house to clear out. It was normal for the family to run errands after the house was cleaned on Saturday. Mama always had to take care of business. Once gone, and the house was empty, I had my imaginary stage. The stage was my shower.*

In the shower stall, I could be me. It was the place where I expressed myself comfortably. I did not worry about what others may say regarding my musical expression. I loved my stage. I kept it a secret. God gave me a voice that could comfort lost souls coupled with a place to practice my vocal talent. Free Will looked at Angel strangely. Angel said, *Girl, I would sing my songs. Sometimes I would stay in the bathroom for hours after my shower and just sing and sing and sing and sing. My favorite song is "Amazing Grace." I loved to take my time, hit the notes in a way that I never heard another person hit and thank God in complete amazement for the gift birthed right out of my pain.*

Looking sad, Angel thought about what happened that made her feel dirty. It was time to move forward and grow from the dirt sprinkled in life's experience to the destination to bring forth deliverance through song. She continued the conversation after a moment of silence.

Everything was perfect. I graduated from high school, sang in the choir, but looked forward to my performances in the shower. From age eight to the present, I practiced and perfected my gift. This particular Saturday, I entered a warm bathroom because my mother readied herself later than usual to prepare for the day's outing. I really looked forward to entering a warm shower because my vocal chords respond better under the steam heat.

The coast was clear. Everybody went their separate way, and I entered the shower to sing the song of my life. Then it happened. The worst nightmare that could possibly happen in the daytime occurred; the thing that gave me goose bumps to think about. My mother burst in the room and caught me in mid-breath. She screamed with excitement because she always thought that I could carry a tune, but she had no idea. "Angel, get dressed," my mother yelled. "Come out of there now." I thought to myself. What was I to do? Do I stay in the shower? Do I stay in my comfort zone? Do I come off the imaginary stage and sing for my mother in the same manner that I sang to the shower curtain? An unwanted visitor, my mother, had invaded my private performance.

My mind was spinning. I was thinking: is the God in the sanctuary of my bathroom ready to stand with me outside of my comfort zone? God gave me a private place to rehearse for five years. God gave me a predictable mother that afforded me time to practice around her regimented schedule. God gave me confidence to sing my heart out in the shower. I get it, my favorite song "Amazing Grace" was His counsel in my restless soul.

Out of the shower singing for my mother, I was free to tell her the entire story that was rooted in pain. Pain brought on by the inappropriate behavior that I experienced by the hands of a former neighbor from the age of seven to ten-years-old. Rescued by my mother from my shame at age fifteen gave meaning to why it was important to sing alone. Singing in the shower washed away the nasty sweat that covered my body because of the sexual abuse experienced by a neighborhood friend. The singing made my insides feel happy. At fifteen years old, it was time for my mother to hear and know the truth about all the bad things that happened to me.

My mother called the police. The neighbor received a twenty-five year sentence for his crime. After the sentencing, my mother said, "Anything a grown-up did to me sexually was not my fault." A violation of trust must not rest in my spirit to make me a victim of my circumstance. I felt safe by my mother's action, years of counseling, and understanding the healing power of God. Free Will looked into Angel's eyes, and with tears streaming down, she thanked her for sharing her wonderful triumph over pain.

Angel entered the stage and the roar of the crowd was breathtaking. The roar washed away the past pain as the warm shower once did when her voice was a secret. Angel's vocal execution is a love walk with God, graced by a soulful expression, rescinded by the healing power of the Holy Spirit. Angel is a gospel jazz artist who opens every session with "Amazing Grace."

Before beginning the next song, Angel looked at the door. A member of the security staff entered the room with obvious intent. He came to watch her. Excitement filled the room but only he and Angel knew who he came to see. Their eyes met. He mouthed the words, "Hello again." Her eyes said, "Hello to you, too." Angel's prayers to God now answered, was confirmed by the cool breeze that rested on both of them.

Angel's Song

Power gained
A secret released
Forgive…
    Live…
        Thrive…
The abusers grip died
"Babe it is over now"
Love language is sweet
Scares mount into strength
Make possible future romantic intent
        The Chorus sings…
            Song birds' jazzy song
            Soothe
            Heartbreak's cloud is gone
            Angel watching me from on high
            Pain of shame gone
            Subside

CHAPTER TWO

The Truth About the Lie I Live

*"But speaking the truth in love, may grow up into him in all things,
which is the head, even Christ."*
Ephesians 4:15 (KJV)

Brock Jordan

ANGEL TOOK UNDER HER WING a new friend named Brock Jordan. Brock came along as a new addition to the neighborhood at a time in Angel's life when her secret revealed itself to her mom. Two years her senior, Brock entered Clark High School in the junior class with a ninth grader, Angel, as a confidant ready to show him the ropes. Brock, welcomed by Angel as the brother she wished she had, was confirmed by the cool breeze that rested on each of them. Nobody really knew where Brock lived in the neighborhood; Angel did not care.

Brock often stayed around to offer his help with the dishes. He helped lift heavy things, he moved and/or carried heavy items around Angel's house. Her mom in turn filled a nurturing role Brock did not receive within his family unit. Brock also started having long talks with Poppa, Angel's grandfather, who had lived with them since Angel could remember. Poppa and Brock hit it off the first time they met. Brock noticed that he and Poppa only conversed when they were alone, but that made the conversations all the more special. It was "men only" time when they sat on the porch together.

Poppa had a glow about him and a way to make words read like a picture in his mind. Talking about his home, Nigeria,

Poppa brought to life the richness of the Nigerian culture. Particularly fond of Lyan (pounded yam), Dodo (Fried Plantains), and Efo (vegetable soup), Poppa explained the dishes in such detail that Brock could smell it as well as see it in his mind. Brock wanted seconds before he had firsts. Poppa's approval of Brock supported Mom Johnson's decision to make Brock an official member of the Johnson family.

Mom Johnson saw Brock as a big brother to Angel and a grandson to Poppa. She reflected on how Brock would talk with Poppa late into the evening, not wanting to go home, but longing to hold tight with every word Poppa spoke. Brock sat on the porch for hours listening to Poppa talk about the "good old days." The rolling melody of hums, head nodding and back slapping made for a man's territory of prose not espoused by women.

Poppa was always open and honest about his past, but Brock was not comfortable pontificating in honest dialog; he was comfortable listening. Brock held back details exposed in the chronic neglect and abandonment that draped a dark shadow of his past. Brock felt guilty because he was not forthright about his background, but could not see past the pain he experienced as a child to tell this wonderful person everything. Ashamed by the manner in which he had to lie, cheat, and steal to survive, Brock portrayed himself as a happy person, but the truth was he was sad inside.

There was a tape looping in Brock's memory regarding how his family could not afford rent. The vivid color surround sound video in brilliant 3D animation exhibited the gritty insight of Brock's suffering. It reminded him of the delicious puss rats stole from his feet as he slept at night on the floor in the vacant row house called home. It was during the day that his bright

smile and intelligence covered up his pain. How could he tell
Poppa how broken he felt? Would Poppa hold it against him
because he did not tell the truth from the start? What would he
think if he knew that every six months his family had to move to
a new neighborhood, new school, new life, and new friends?
How would the truth about the lie he lived help his current
situation with this family he loves?

Poppa understood an unstable life was the course of the
day for Brock. He knew Brock's dilemma because he had his
own past to deal with. Squatting in vacant houses with drug
addicts, rats, and rodents taught Brock the importance of a
shower. Brock prayed and got a job in a local health club. Poppa
knew that working in the local health club doing laundry, was the
employment that provided Brock the way to cleanliness. He
believed in the saying that "Cleanliness is next to Godliness."
Brock did not have to explain "his lie" to Poppa; Poppa knew
about the lie, its resolution, and Brock's destiny. Brock did not
have to confess; Poppa knew about his past and welcomed him
to be part of the Johnson family future.

Brock resembled Poppa—easy on the eyes with perfect
gentleman-like charm. His deep dark skin and pearly white smile,
in direct contrast to Angel's skin tone, matched closely to that of
Mom Johnson and Poppa. Angel's mom use to tease Brock by
saying, "I think you are the perfect candidate for a toothpaste
commercial. Now get out there and make us some money." They
would all laugh because deep down they all knew it was true.

On the surface, it seemed none of life's concerns could
possibly touch Brock because he handled himself wonderfully in
a fashion-forward manner. Many of his fashions were obtained
from items acquired from the health club lost and found box.
Thus, the quality of the items found reflected the taste of the

upper middle class clientèle. The stability of the health club employment eliminated the need for Brock to steal for survival. He enjoyed the freedom that being honest brings. No longer having to look over his shoulders and try to remember the lies he told was a plus. The only shame he carried was regarding his impoverished living environment.

*****

A masterful silent communicator, Brock never had to say one word to get his point across to onlookers. One day, Casey pushed Angel down and hurt her badly. Angel knew it would be necessary to fight Casey even though there was no chance of beating this giant of an opponent. The time had come; she was prepared to take her "beat down." Knowing others would witness the event, forced Angel to take a firm stance so others would not try the same behavior. Angel had a straight-back firm-faced defiance that only happens when a person cannot take being harassed anymore. She geared up to get in at least one good lick, understanding the consequence would result in bodily harm. Angel thought as she approached the battle ground, "When I am in my crazy mood I will pick up a chair to hit an enemy to ensure others know if they mess with Angel, they will pay the cost." Brock internalized the entire scene. He was not about to let anyone harm Angel.

With the determination of a heroic big brother, Brock stepped in to help before Angel had a chance to engage in battle. He entered the battle ground, stared into the eyes of the assailant as if to say, "You missed your chance to harm Angel, I am in the family now." Casey got the message loud and clear, Brock did not utter one word. It was that deep. His silence seemed to strongly say, "I will break your face in and embarrass your stare." That motivated Casey to establish an instantaneous, meaningful friendship with Angel. Brock's silent communication penetrated Casey's skull, reached common sense, then motivated the "do the right thing" part of the brain to take over. Casey backed off. Brock's approach to battle electrified the crowd that gathered to witness the event. His approach to battle was more effective than yelling, screaming, and using four letter words. Big brothers, larger than life, can back off the most sinister opponent. Brock took his role as a big brother very seriously.

The aftermath of the Casey altercation gave Brock the courage to open up about his life. He felt the desire to tell Angel and Poppa the truth—the truth about how he wore parental neglect as the veil of abuse fueled by the by-product of drug abuse. His parents' drug abuse resulted in emotional abuse experienced by parents who could only work to get the next high. Brock's home consisted of vacant buildings that housed crack heads, drug dealers, prostitutes, and rats. Angel felt bad for Brock. Poppa already knew the truth. He was waiting for Brock to reveal it in his own time.

It was a heavy day filled with open confessions, truths, and sadness. Angel and Brock were sitting in the kitchen trying to take it all in. Mom Johnson had made a meal of Poppa's favorites that had now become Brock's favorites. There was a sense of purpose in the air. The meal time did not include the usual jovial conversation. Poppa never ate with them, but Brock never thought it strange. Mom Johnson entered the kitchen with a very serious face. She said, "I was sitting on the porch talking to Poppa and we both agreed that, Brock, we would like you to become an official member of the Johnson family." Brock looked at Mom Johnson and Angel, struggling not to let tears that were already streaming down inside of his soul come out of his eyes. Unable to contain himself, Brock put his head on the table in the crease of his arm and cried like a new born baby. The dream that someone grounded in goodness would want him to become part of the family never seemed possible, but now it was true. Brock could not look up. Mom Johnson and Angel sat in chairs on each side of him, put their arms around him, and cried equally as hard. After ten minutes of crying, Mom Johnson said, "I take that as a YES." Brock said through his tears, "Yes, ma'am ."

Mom Johnson knew of the arrest of Brock's parent and knew it would not be long before he was placed in a foster home. She contacted the Department of Social Services about becoming a foster care home for Brock. The home study, scheduled to begin the day after Brock agreed to be part of the Johnson family, made everything official. Poppa informed Mom Johnson that "a new life call was in order" for Brock.

CHAPTER THREE

A New Life Order

"When I say to a wicked man, 'You will surely die,' and you do not warn him or speak out to dissuade him from his evil ways in order to save his life, that wicked man will die for his sin, and I will hold you accountable for his blood."
Ezekiel 3:18 (NIV)

Brock

A S BROCK'S NEW FAMILY, MOM Johnson, Poppa and Angel agreed to provide him protection, food, clothing, and a safe place to crash at the end of the day, coupled with plenty of love and affection. The standards of the Johnson family unit rested well with Brock. Brock was very happy about his new home. Prior to accepting his new living arrangement with the Johnson household, he did not see the harm of joining a gang. Compared to living in a neglectful home laced with emotional abuse, Brock thought at one point, that living with a gang was better than living in a vacant house. Mom Johnson, Poppa and Angel changed that way of thinking for him. They represented a family unit who took the time to get to know and love Brock before they invited him into the home to live. In addition to housing, the Johnson family believed in going to church and trusting God. Brock began his formal introduction to understanding the ways of living as a Christian.

Reading the Bible offered new insights. It opened Brock's intellect to new inquiries: a new purpose for life, a new reason to make something of his life because Jesus suffered, bled, and died that we might have life. That intrigued Brock the most about giving his life to Christ. A photographic memory allowed Brock to recite every passage he had ever read. With exceptional comprehension abilities, Brock understood completely the magnitude of his gift. Because he moved every six months, Brock never was an academic stand out in school before attending Clark High School. High school classes, Bible classes, and life's lessons to ponder from Mom Johnson, demonstrated for Brock the magnitude of the Lord's goodness.

Once enrolled in the high school zoned for Angel's neighborhood, Brock fell in love with track and field. His ability to run fast, exceeded by one individual, Rome, made him an important member of the track team. For the first time in his life, Brock was happy about his surroundings, school, and friends. However, when introduced to people, Brock was aloof about explaining his past. He never discussed his parents. Looking back, his sixteenth birthday represented a memory of regrets that deeply lacked the celebration afforded such a milestone event. Angel looked forward to the celebration Mom Johnson planned for Brock's eighteenth birthday because they all agreed that it had to be great.

Brock had a very successful junior year in high school. He was on the four by one hundred relay team, he received straight "As" in all of his classes, and all the girls wanted to be close to him. He was happy, felt loved and adored. Brock was feeling sad when he said, "My life is a lie." Angel sat still, speechless because she could see through the pain in his eyes. A trustworthy brother-sister bond felt good to both of them. Brock opened the conversation with a confession of how difficult it was for him growing up in a neglectful, emotionally abusive family prior to living with the Johnson family.

Brock said, "Though I moved on, the feeling of neglect stays with me. I still feel like I need to run from the authorities and protect myself while feeling very safe here at the same time. Always moving from place to place, eating what the rats did not get to first makes me feel guilty because I am doing better now. What do I do about the people who do not have food?" Angel replied, "Be successful, Brock. Do all you can to make a better life for yourself so that you can make a better life for others. Please do not let any of those chicken head girls at school try to make you their baby's daddy." Brock felt good about what Angel said. He felt comfortable that if he said anything to Angel, she would pray to God for help. One thing Brock sincerely believed, and that was that Prayer works.

Sitting on the porch late one evening, Poppa saw the anguished look on Brock's face, and knew it was important that Brock know the motivating factor that made it overwhelmingly easy to welcome him into the Johnson household. "The truth of the matter," Poppa said, "I lost my son, Mom Johnson's brother, to a gang of leers, thieves and drug dealers. They confronted him the way I saw them confront you across the street and on the corner. I have never met a young man as bright as you and it is time for me to give back. We trusted God to get us to a place where we could open our home to a young man like you in spite of Angel's disturbing experience because we see the special bond you share. I witnessed Angel share with you in a manner that she would not do with her counselor. I watched her prepare to fight a bully rather than run because you helped her develop confidence.

"The gang confronted my son with a bullet to his head when he decided he did not want to live like that anymore. You experienced what you had to in life, so we could heal through establishing a relationship with you and you can heal through establishing a relationship with us. Prior to the bullet in my son's head, there were alibis and false stories I told to keep my son away from the scene of the crime. My son lived a lie disguised as a saved church-going, young man. The public truth was, my son was an enemy of the state. Since your application is on the head table of the local gang leader, I want to do whatever possible to provide safety in a law-abiding household. You are my son, and I am your Poppa. Let your past pains heal your truth so you will stop living a lie. Brock, you are a Johnson now." Brock felt better as he hugged Poppa as a five-year old boy would hug his daddy.

*****

Now that Brock decided to become a positive example of what it means to do right as a member of the Johnson family, he was motivated to consider attending the different colleges that were attempting to recruit him on the basis of his outstanding SAT scores. Brock said, "The gang of colleges represents a society that agrees to provide a place to lay my head, three meals a day, and a family of teachers, counselors, and friends that would support my successful matriculation. The college attendance represents the type of truth that will support the legitimate lifestyle inclusive of positive standards that represent who I want to become." Brock's truth is that, he wanted the lifestyle of an overachieving college student.

The idea of joining a gang once felt good to Brock. At this stage in his life, the only family that felt right was the Johnson family, which consisted of Angel, Poppa and Mom Johnson. Brock wanted to embrace the household to engage the possibilities of his life's future. Brock secretly understood that being around Angel's family would give him the freedom to open his heart and not live in the lie of being okay while living in neglect and emotional abuse, where on a bad day, his parents would call him terrible names and tell him he would never make anything of his life. They would make him watch their sexual acts because they knew it repulsed him. He would no longer live the lie of his past, but relished in the truth that life holds great possibilities. This truth brought him to rest in the bosom of the Johnson household.

Brock delighted in the plans for the positive direction of his life. He also had a crush that he held secret. Not even Angel knew. In time he would let Angel know, but until that time it was between him and God.

Defending Angel from Casey gave Brock purpose. The truth of the matter is, up until that time and space on the battlefield with Casey the giant, Brock never felt as though he had purpose for his life. "Angel," Brock said, "I do not want you to look up to a wandering soul." Angel replied, "I thank God you wandered because you ended up here as the brother I never had. Your past brought you into my life. I celebrate God Who brought you here. Please do not be sad about the turn of events that brought you here to be my brother. I love you and pray your purpose here brings you happiness." With a smile on his face, Brock said, "It feels good having a stable God-fearing family and home to live in. I love all of you and do not want to ever do anything wrong to mess things up."

CHAPTER FOUR

The Last Shall Be First

But many that are first shall be last; and the last shall be first.
Matthew 19:30 (KJV)

Rome Augusta

RAISED BY HIS GRANDMOTHER, ROME Augusta was in a very protective home. It was difficult for him to get permission to participate in martial arts like his cousins. His grandmother took her parental role seriously. Unfortunately, her energy level did not allow for the active lifestyle enjoyed by today's young people. Grandma would always say, "I thank God for you Rome, but I don't have the energy to run you all around town. Maybe when you get a little older I will let you get involved in martial arts." That possibility gave Rome hope that he would have an opportunity to enjoy the martial art class of his favorite cousin, Sir, who was a third degree black belt.

By age twelve, Grandma released Rome to participate with his cousin in marital arts class. Always a gentleman, Sir was an excellent role model for Rome. However, there was one thing about Sir, Rome did not embrace fully. Sir treated women with the utmost care and dignity. Rome did not like that at all. He felt like if women were supposed to be a man's queen, why did he get beat by his mother nightly. His mother said every time she beat him, "I must beat the Hell out of you before it leaps into me." The nightly ritual continued until one day Rome's Grandma witnessed the terrible behavior when she dropped in to visit. Rome was five years old standing in the bathroom butt naked as his mother beat him with the belt breaking his skin to expose "the white meat." Turning black and blue was the gift he received on the nights when the beatings were less intense.

Rome later learned that was the beginning of the end for his "normal" home life. His mother could not effectively answer Grandma's questions of: "why are you beating this child?" Rome's mother broke down, curled up into a fetal position on the floor, and cried like a baby. The daughter, the mother, the only person who loved Rome was committed to a mental care facility that night. Rome had been with his Grandma ever since.

As escapism from the many valleys of life, Rome used violent video games as an outlet and disrespect for all females. By age sixteen he loved to pull girls in, watch them fall for him, verbally degrade them, and watch them fall away. He disguised his game plan with a smile, well-toned body and exceptional athleticism. He was a high school track star. His rock hard voice of reason, and confidant was Sir. Sir kept it "real" and chastised Rome's unacceptable behavior. Rome received the chastisement as love.

Sir, a role model who overcame a tremendous amount of sadness, found peace in the love of his life, Lysa. Some people thought he was not attracted to women. That was far from the truth. The fact is, Sir, at one point, felt uncomfortable approaching women. Lysa changed all of that with her bright smile and understanding spirit. Sir fell in love with Lysa and vowed to marry the most beautiful woman he had ever laid eyes on.

Lysa came from a long line of ministers of the gospel. Lysa's up-bringing afforded her opportunities to read the intentions of a person before they were ready to articulate their intent themselves. She could see straight into the intent of Sir's humble, giving spirit the second she laid eyes on him. Love at first sight would describe how they felt about each other. Lysa loved the man Sir was destined to be. Lysa experienced the emotional support when she met Sir that never was available in former relationships.

Sir died in a car accident on his way for the wedding tuxedo fitting. Devastated by Sir's death, Rome curled up on the bathroom floor and cried like he had seen his mother do many years ago. The accident did not cause Lysa to question God; she thanked God for the chance to know what it feels like to participate in a God-ordained relationship. After Sir's death, Lysa vowed to wear her wedding ring, purchased by Sir, until a man of equal caliber came along who represented a purity found in the experience of falling in love with a man who purposefully waited for his first love. Sir was that man.

Sir's martial arts trophies and awards spread throughout his apartment. It had always been Rome's secret to put his martial awards throughout his own apartment. To facilitate that possibility, Sir, both financially and emotionally sponsored Rome's quest to become a black belt martial artist. Now at eighteen years old Rome completed the final phase of his black belt testing that was to take place the week after Sir's funeral. Sir would have turned twenty-eight years old on the date of his funeral. The very sad occasion turned Rome's focus into a downward spiral.

Sir's guidance and love was so taken for granted by Rome that when Sir went on to be with the Lord, Rome could not bear to move forward in the marital arts because he was used to being second to Sir. Rome was use to being last and could not fathom the possibility of moving to the first position. Rome's comfort in the coverage of Sir's shadow allowed him to know that he was not alone.

Angel went to Sir's funeral and stopped by Sir's parents' home after the funeral to comfort and assure Rome that everything would be all right. Rome cried in Angel's arms. He could not hold back the public tears any longer. The reality that his lifelong friend and cousin left him alone made Rome find pity in the fact that he had to deal with his internal demons without his cousin's guidance.

Angel reminded Rome that it was all right to continue to live and to allow all that Sir taught him to live through him. She said, "Let your standing in position represent strength, power, and purpose that benefits others from operating behind a leader." Rome had two completely different sides of his personality. One side of his behavior was positive. It reflected behavior he witnessed from Sir. This behavior was always prepared to operate front and center to draw compliments from the room. Now it was Rome's turn to be "an example," to "lead the way," to "represent a brighter hope for tomorrow." He was ready to take the lead. Taking the lead came with the responsibility to trust God to lead and operate in a manner that gives God glory.

The opportunity to move forward in life was possible, yet Rome presented himself as upright to his boys while in secret he wanted to make others feel as bad as he did on the inside. The question that was before him was: would he try to do right by people or continue to have abusive behavior toward females? Would he appear publicly to be one way, but have evil intent, or would he purpose himself to be upright and truthful? Rome had always been second to Sir, now was he ready to lead? Was he ready to be first?

CHAPTER FIVE

*"I will walk about in freedom, for I have sought out
your precepts."*
Psalm 119:45 (NIV)

Freedom Wilson

ALL KNEW FREEDOM WILSON A.K.A, Free Will. A poet, clothed with "thankfulness" and "a praise the Lord mentality," she and her mom were heroic survivors who escaped from the abusive grip of her stepfather. Born in Lagos, Nigeria, Free Will was the apple of her father's eye, and the motivational drive for her mother to seek a better life. By age two, an unfortunate accident at work killed her father. Her mom, Anne, left her grief in Nigeria and moved to America looking for a better life for her daughter. Free Wilson's mother married Matthew Wilson who officially adopted Free Will at the age of five. The better life in America was picture perfect; at least Anne thought it was at the time.

The fourth child of seven sisters and two brothers, Free Will's mom, Anne, had an opportunity to marry a wonderful American man who treated her and Free Will like princesses. Her family unit was picture perfect until the stepfather's brother, Griffin, came to live with them. Griffin was a very nice person on the surface, but underneath there was a soul of a molester. At twelve years of age, Free Will filled his ungodly sexual fantasies for several months. Griffin came into her bedroom after everyone had gone to sleep offering a warm glass of milk. Upon drinking the milk, Free Will noticed the room had darkened; shame came in to intrude her purity with lustful intent. The smell on her private area made the morning shower ritual the only chance to wash away the previous evening's horrible nightmare. Free Will's mom and stepfather did not know about Griffin's deviant behavior.

Several months after the sexual abuse began, Anne noticed how Free Will stepped back whenever Griffin entered the room. Something felt strange—off kilter. With no evidence to support her gut feeling, Anne began to put the pieces together. Free Will would use any excuse to stay the night at her friend's house. Anne watched Free Will keep her distance from Griffin, stay away from home as much as possible and thought it was time to confront Free Will with "the question."

The confrontation started with "the question"— has someone touched you in your private area? The answer resulted in uncontrollable crying, trembling, and tremendous shame. Free Will told her mother of how her step-uncle, Griffin, came into her room at nights with a glass of warm milk and got on top of her. Immediately, her mother called the police, filed a complaint, packed her daughter up, left her husband, the state, and moved to Baltimore. With no forwarding address, or contact information, a new beginning was in store for the duo. Receiving family support from her four sisters who lived in America, Free Will's mom soon found a job, a new home, and a new start.

Free Will never looked back—only forward. Touching her body was out of the question; only people who could stimulate her intellect had a chance to enter her comfort zone. Words on paper spoke louder than the voice of the abuser. The more she wrote poetry, the more the voice in her past quieted. As she shared poetry with audiences, the voice from the past, along with its associated video that played continually in her head, went into the archives of forgiveness. Birthed from her pain was power, a dynamic God-fearing purpose that gave audiences cause to listen, ponder, grow, and gain determination to fight the enemy without gloves.

Free Will was a willing participant in the army of the Lord. This Blood-washed, fired-up, baptized believer in Jesus Christ focused on the mark of the higher calling. It was her motto that "God is not only proud about the way she rocked the crowd, God was also pleased with her sneeze." In other words, it is in the likeness of God that Free Will strove to emulate. Though nowhere near perfect, her imperfection rested in the shadow of God's perfection.

Free Will was not a preacher called to stand up in the pulpit to preach the gospel. She was a soldier, a servant, a great friend, a willing participant positioned to stand with the lost and speak God's truth. Representing the highest state of happiness and contentment, Free Will could be identified as a beatitude; she reflected behavior that was pleasing to God. Her life was a sermon that was cultivated by her Sunday morning presence in the pew. Free Will represented freedom. Her freedom flowed in the Will of God.

Kasha was the only person who held that special "sister girl" spot in Free Will's heart. She had many friends, but Kasha was a permanent fixture in Free Will's home. Kasha was aware of Free Will's secret dream that one of the guy's on the Clark High School track team, Brock, would step into her space and fill it with his beautiful smile. It had never been Free Will's intent to have a relationship with someone still in high school while she was entering senior year in college, but there was something very special about his approach to life. Trusted to keep the secret hush-hush, Kasha was glad to play the role of number one friend.

Words from the Bible fueled Free Will's thought patterns in reflective rhymes embraced by poetry spit on Friday and Saturday nights at local poetry readings. Free Will's morning commune with God and her pastor's Sunday sermons, seasoned with psalms and hymns, played back in her mind. Her peace provoking practices that opened her up to the positive attributes of a silver lining, wonderful blends of southern blues and Mom's cookin', belt out the birthing pains that carried her poetic lyrics. Free Will's gospel mixes of southern blues blended with Nigerian rhythms hurt when the moment was wrong and sound sweet when the moment was right. Her rhymes reminded audiences of the meaningful correction God uses to move each of us into the path of His healing power.

CHAPTER SIX

The Oil and Water Mix

Then I will let her waters settle and make her streams flow like oil,
declares the Sovereign LORD.
Ezekiel 32:14 (NIV)

Free Will & Alex

IF YOU EVER HAD A teacher who "loved you enough to tell you the truth", usually in the beginning you may have thought that teacher had crossed the line because what they said made you feel uncomfortable—that was Free Will and Alex. In the beginning of their destiny together, their relationship was an "oil and water" experience. There was just something about each of them that did not jell. A good shake, by the grace of God, in concert with a little spice of the past and present experiences, blended as a great salad dressing for life. The teacher and apprentice solidified into a loving grateful-to-God relationship. Delighted to become a life coach, Free Will agreed to sponsor Alex's transition to America.

Alex, Free Will's first cousin, was Auntie Amara's first born son. Amara is the sixth child of the nine siblings. Alex came to America under the cover of night with the support from his family to become a better person. Chosen as the perfect mentor for Alex, Free Will felt blessed to have the chance to help her cousin find his way. A selection by the Oni sisters to be Alex's mentor came after a meeting of the seven sisters. Anne was excited to give back to her siblings after they helped her so much in the past. Free Will developed a plan to make sure Alex would find his way to reside in peace. Her mother, Anne, was proud to take on this responsibility as well.

The four Oni sisters, who lived in America, pooled their money to support Anne while she was starting a new life in Baltimore for her daughter. Now, it was Anne's turn to help Amara, the only Oni sister residing in London many miles away from family. The remaining siblings, one sister, and her two brothers, resided in Nigeria and ran the family businesses.

Upon arrival in the States, Alex quickly learned his new American accent. In an attempt to leave the past behind, Alex identified Maryland as his state of origin. Alex enrolled as a junior in Clark High School within Free Will's school district. Once enrolled into the local high school as a junior, the students had no reason to make exception to Alex's historical accounts.

Alex had a secret. He longed for the liberty to come and go and not to be a slave to the cravings. Alex's cravings called him to attend places that embrace the beat of sexually explicit dancing—the thumping to the beat of X-rated music with lyrics that did not meet FCC standards. Alex's cravings were the same as those that make an addict itch. Alex's cravings were completely off limits for day light performance. The pain of his home life pushed him to seek relief in the strip club. Free Will's goal was to fill the pain with celebrations of life that enlighten the mind.

Alex became part of Free Will's poetic flow. Alex's tumultuous life, never openly discussed, was ever present. Head nods without benefit of comment among the audience of one voice kept his problems within his immediate family unit. His mother knew, however, that outside of the immediate family, help was available to coach a young man back to health. Only a woman who knew his plight, without explanation could do the job of addressing his issues. Free Will was perfect for the job.

Alex was born and raised in London, England. He had a baby face and a full head of curly black hair, black rim eye glasses, and vocal cords that were searching for its grown man octave. His parents adore him deeply. They wanted Alex to be free from the baggage of his experiences. As a result, it was their desire not to leave a paper trail that would allow his experiences to overflow into his present situation. Safety within the family structure in America was the motivation behind them modifying official documents so that he could regain his youthful status as a high school student. Alex was nineteen years old posing as a seventeen year old junior in High School when Free Will stepped in to become his life coach. Free Will, instructed to engage Alex in team sports, did so as part of his rehabilitation process.

Only after a few weeks of intense oversight by Free Will, did Alex want to start doing things differently. He looked forward to the Friday and Saturday night poetry readings. Sitting next to Free Will at Tuesday night Bible study and Sunday morning church service was comfortable; it felt right, it felt like a new beginning. Alex really did not pay attention to the preacher at first, he just noticed how proud Free Will was to have his companionship. Alex was beginning to feel the positivity that takes place in the family unit.

Free Will was saving to purchase the home one block over from her mother. The highlight to affording a home is, the gate to the rear exit of the property was facing the back alley directly across from Free Will's current home with her mother. Alex was excited for Free Will's liberation into her own residence. As a spiritual warrior, she will reside in a home that expanded the territory of her influence. He was happy to be part of her influential sphere.

During the summer, Alex's cravings started lessening. Free Will still kept Alex close. She kept him in the space of very positive people. Of course, none of these people knew Alex's history. Free Will wanted only God to judge Alex's past, not man. Sometimes people try to step in to do God's job and judge one's transgressions. Alex broke away in the middle of the night from an abusive home life. His new life with Free Will and Auntie Anne was moving forward in God's direction.

Uncle Butch was Alex's sports mentor. With Alex as the student and Uncle Butch as the coach, they jointly prepared Alex for running the 100 meter dash with the intent to making sure Alex was in top shape before the start of the track and field season. As a former high school standout in track and field, Uncle Butch took pride in Alex's improved 100 meter dash times. More importantly, Alex took pride in the fact that Uncle Butch was beside him every step of the way.

During tryouts, Uncle Butch read the Scripture Free Will posted on her blog before practice. Praying was not a strong suit for Uncle Butch or Alex, so reading the Scripture aloud as a prayer prepared them before practice. Everybody in the family knew Auntie Anne and Free Will were the prayer warriors. After three weeks of tryouts, the track team roster posted for all to see. Alex made the team. Uncle Butch was as happy as Alex was delighted to see their hard work pay off. That made it all worthwhile.

Alex told Uncle Butch, "When I got on-line, pulled up the track team roster of players and I was on the list, I jumped for joy. For the first time in a long time, I felt like I did something good. I thank God for you, Uncle Butch, Free Will and Auntie Anne. The four by one hundred meter relay team consisted of Brock, Randall, Rome and I. The guy, Rome, has world class speed. Alex thought to himself, I am stoked about running with him. My dream of becoming a member of the track team came true. Finally, I did something that my family could be proud of. Finally, I can see for myself how hard work and perseverance can witness Hope triumph. Thanks again Uncle Butch for everything." With all that said, the announcement was not simply the fact that Alex made the team, but he trusted people to help him achieve his goals.

With the motivation and support by Uncle Butch, Alex became part of the four-by-one-hundred meter relay team. The push and purpose by Uncle Butch provided the foundation for the dream of a better tomorrow. Comfortable that Alex was in good hands, Free Will went away for her senior year in college with the reins turned over to Auntie Anne, Uncle Butch and Cousin Luke to balance out the life lines in place to keep Alex walking the straight and narrow way ordained by God.

Upon arriving in America, Alex did not want to stay with Free Will. In time, however, Alex began to love all that was good about her. What made Free Will so special is the fact that she is "free," and not controlled by anything outside of the Will of God. Expressions of oneness with God embody her existence. The open atmosphere of her home balances the importance of earth, water, and fire. It worked—Alex got it—the past is not in front, but in the memory—all that Alex will forget made room for the promises of tomorrow. Oil and water do mix when the intent is to make a great salad dressing, but it only works if the bottle is shaken. God shakes the bottle during the hour of prayer.

CHAPTER SEVEN

Best Friends

"A man of many companions may come to ruin, but there is a friend who sticks closer than a brother."
Proverbs 18:24 (NIV)

Kasha Brown

KASHA BROWN HAS EXCEPTIONAL BEAUTY with a rock hard video vixen body. She is the envy of many. Free Will's best friend, Kasha, has made a name for herself in the world of music videos, gaining celebrity by gliding across the floor to crawl up the wall with the best of them. She and Free Will go way back to the days when they were playmates in nursery school.

Kasha's phone rings off the hook now that she appeared in the number one rap artist's video as his love interest. It is her prayer to take on a more serious love interest—not a role. "The film is in the can." It is confirmed by director, Martin, as Kasha is currently viewed as more than just another body; she is now a "love interest"—in a rap video. Realizing it is just a fantasy interest, the power of video media may expose Kasha to the respectable movie directors. Consumed with people's opinion of her, Kasha depends on Free Will to remind her that she is a child of God.

Kasha's physical presence resulted in plenty of attention from men, but all she wants is what Free Will has. Free Will is lyrically "correct," "proper," "in-tune," "lethal." In Kasha's mind, Free Will's mind is what attracts a person to be part of her inner circle. Kasha knows it is her body that makes her so powerful.

At least that is what she has allowed herself to believe.

Free Will has a mind that can unpeel a thought before others have digested its meaning. Free from the stereotypes that say you have to be a certain size to be acceptable, Free Will is empowered by the presence of God to obtain the attention from men without having to take her clothes off as Kasha has done on many occasions. Free Will celebrates a rock hard relationship with God. Kasha celebrates her rock hard body.

Kasha is the sort of friend that Free Will thanks God for because Kasha is faithful, real and will tell you like it is even if you do not want to hear it. Free Will prays to have her special Kasha friendship and does not feed into the assessment others have regarding her friend. In the past, Free Will has had to let friends go because they became envious about what God was doing in her life. It is different with Kasha. She understands the heartbeat of Free Will's past. Thus, Free Will's sometimes distant behavior is accepted as par for the course because the pain of the past gives Free Will cause to rest for long periods.

Those friends who were not around when Free Will was molested by her step uncle do understand, that time alone, prayer, meditation and lyrics thrown into the air are done so she continues to find reason to live and celebrate life. Friends who do not realize the origin of Free Will's thickness was the over indulgence in pancakes for breakfast, pasta for lunch and fast food dinner plus dessert offered a major comfort for the pain. Now that Free Will is grown, with lyrical engagements up and down the coast, the craving for carbohydrates has lessened. Love no longer indulged in excess calories; it is in the pronouncement of lyrics after fasting, praying, and having meditative time with God. For Free Will, Kasha provides motivation to eat to live and not live to eat. Since being in the company of Kasha as a young adult,

Free Will has taken off thirty-pounds in the course of one-year. At that rate, she will be at her goal weight loss of ninety-pounds in two-years and that is okay with her.

CHAPTER EIGHT

The enemy boasted,
'I will pursue, I will overtake them.
I will divide the spoils;
I will gorge myself on them.
I will draw my sword
and my hand will destroy them.'
Exodus 15:9 (NIV)

True Colors Come Out

ANGEL WAS SITTING AT THE window in Auntie Anne's house the day of Free Will's cousin's high school graduation party. The truth of the matter was, her cousin Alex is somewhat of a mystery to anyone not on the track team. As a member of the track team, Brock was invited to the party and Angel attended with Brock.

The back yard was crowded and the party was jumping. Angel was sitting in a seat next to the stairs where both Rome and Kasha were sitting. She knew Rome because he would come to the house and hang out with Brock. There was something about him that Angel did not like, but Brock liked him. So Angel kept her negative thoughts about Rome to herself. Kasha, on the other hand was infamous because of the below standard videos that exposed too much of her body, although things were looking up based on her latest video presentation. She was sexy and covered and on her way to becoming a real actor. It was apparent to Angel that both Rome and Kasha did not notice her sitting beside them because they were scheming right in her ear shot. She could hear the entire conversation.

Rome wanted to do whatever it took to win Free Will's heart. Kasha, in turn, wanted Rome to put in a good word for her with Brock so that she may have a possibility to win his heart to engage in exotic episodes. Torn because of Free Will's secret crush on Brock, Kasha wanted to steal Free Will's secret before it becomes a reality.

There is a problem with Kasha's scheme because Brock is feelin' Free Will too. Brock never had one face-to-face conversation with Free Will, but he had many in his dreams. He wants Free Will to feel his presence while he continues to enjoy her positive vibe and witness her potential. He desires to obtain placement on Free Will's short list of potential male suitors. However, Rome is watching and waiting for his opportunity to move in on Free Will. For Rome, Brock is an opponent who must be defeated.

The Brock-Free Will connection are two people waiting to get in the middle of undeclared feelings—attempting to up-root the plant of forever before the roots can be planted into declared love. Brock and Free Will are unknowing participants in the center of a love affair that has yet to take place. It is in the envy of what Free Will has today and not what she had to go through to get where she is today that Kasha feels the need to get in between the Brock-Free Will dream. Kasha is hiding the truth from her friend. She wants her friend's secret crush.

Angel was interested in Brock's well being and could see Kasha coming from a mile away. Angel thought, "The best way to kill a snake is to cut off its head." She went to Kasha looking for direct answers to direct questions. Angel said to Kasha, "Why would you risk hurting your best friend by messing with the man of her dreams? Why is it so important for you to stop Free Will from finding happiness with Brock?" Kasha said, "I don't want anybody to come along to fill the void that I fill in Free Will's life. I want to be Free Will's VBF. If I have to get Brock out of the way to do so, so be it." Angel said to Kasha, "You are suffering from the green eyed monster 'envy' because you see something in someone else you wish you had for yourself. Stop it before you lose your friend. You should support Free Will in her pursuit of happiness." Kasha said, "Do you and I will do me. This conversation is over. Peace out!" Kasha is not a friend, but a frienemy. A frienemy is a person who is envious and competitive with very close friends. In some ways, they can be the best confidant and trusted associate. In other ways, they may seek to tear out the fabric of every relationship that is positive and meaningful in your life.

Rome came back from the restroom and could tell that Kasha was agitated. "Angel wants me to back off of Brock," Kasha said. "It's not her business what you do," Rome insisted. "Everyone can see that Brock is infatuated by Free Will." "That's not my problem," Rome replied. The word infatuated invoked the spirit of competition in Rome. Rome thought to himself, *"I can't take another perfect "A" list Hollywood dream girl. Free Will has an awesome presence that makes me want to steal another man's dream. I want Brock's dream—Free Will."* It was from a safe distance that Brock made it very clear to his boys that Free Will is his "Dream." Free Will was in the "hands off" category. At least in Brock's mind, his desires took Free Will off the market. Now all he had to do was to get permission from Free Will to make her a reality and not a dream. Rome was not buying any of that. "The best man wins," is what Rome said to Kasha as he continued to plot to win Free Will's heart. "Getting what we want is all that matters," Rome said as Kasha agreed. They continued to party with the guests as Angel prayed for direction.

*****

Brock was invited to Alex's graduation party, which delighted Free Will though she kept a respectable distance with her inviting eyes. Other than saying "Hello," Brock had never uttered more than one word in Free Will's direction. Free Will liked everything good about his shyness. Brock, in turn, had never been shy about approaching any female, actually there are many in line waiting for a chance to go out with him. Free Will is different—she is the impossible dream made possible. She is the light at the end of the tunnel. She is out of his league. Brock prays that college will be the training camp that he may prepare to graduate into her league and if God is willing, she will be there for him upon graduation.

Angel has always been a little sister to Free Will and was invited to the graduation party as a guest. Free Will understood fully that there was no love between Kasha and Angel. She attributed the tension to sibling rivalry. Call it what you want, but they could not stand the sight of one another. Angel felt a sense of evil intent when it came to Kasha and was out to get to the bottom of her ill- feelings at the party.

This new level of healing had given Alex purpose to look ahead and not behind at past mistakes. Embracing Philippians 3:14, Alex said, he will "… press toward the mark for the prize of the high calling of God in Christ Jesus." With suitcase in hand, purpose chiseled in his heart and a desire to fulfill his dream, Alex proceeded with a smile towards his destination beyond the Boston College.

Rome knew he had an image to maintain that was worthy of a world class athlete. He knew that was true, but in spite of the fact that Brock's dream fell outside the boundary from which a world class athlete would engage, he still wanted Brock's dream. In the competition to take the dream, it required Rome to step outside of his comfort zone and make sweet conversation with Free Will in full view of Brock's longing stare.

Randall felt some level of guilt about betting Rome he could not pull Free Will. The intensity of this is causing a strain on Randall's friendship with Brock. Randall wondered out loud, "is a girl off limits if she is another friend's Dream?" Brock's lack of social skills impeded his ability to excel in the area of partaking in charming conversation. Brock believed in God and took this chance to pray to God to make his dream come true.

Prior to designing a strategy to implement a Free Will connection plan, Brock never committed to becoming a friend with any females because of the fear of moving away. Now that moving away was not going to happen, because of his permanent home with Angel, Momma and Poppa, Brock needed to learn how to commit to a relationship in order to make his Dream a reality.

Brock was raised in the streets and knew when an evil plan was about to take place. His instincts, or as the old timers would say, "the Holy Spirit", alerted Brock to the fact that his boy was interested in being more than "just friends" with his Dream. Brock could tell by the way Rome did not encourage him to go after Free Will that it was an open competition to win Free Will's heart.

Rome repeatedly reminded Brock that Free Will was out of his league. That was enough for Brock to know that a plan was in place for Rome to steal his Dream. One thing Brock learned from living on the streets—do not get head strong about having anything that may mess up your living space or food supply.

Nature was going to take its course and Brock was going

to sit back, not say anything or intervene when Rome went after Free Will. It really hurt Brock and all he could think is how, Free Will was his Dream, his brothers were for real and God would control the outcome of this one. Brock made up his mind not to get in God's way. He trusted God—not his boy Rome to do the right thing. Brock's track team mates were the brothers he never had. He was not going to let anyone get in the way of that—not even his Dream. Brock backed off and let the possibility of his Dream die.

CHAPTER NINE

"Your beginnings will seem humble, so prosperous will your future be."
Job 8:7 (NIV)

Alex

ALEX GRADUATED FROM HIGH SCHOOL with top honors. Awarded a scholarship to a college in the city of Boston, Massachusetts, Alex exceeded his own expectations. Free Will was delighted her gifted cousin made the seamless transition to matriculate through an American High School without any hiccups. The Boston City College was located close enough for Alex to return to Free Will's home in Baltimore for weekend visits when workload permitted.

The southern style graduation send-off for Alex in Auntie Anne's back yard required her newly adopted American family to orchestrate the festivities. Uncle Butch came over to clean out the roasting pit for the rack of lamb, prepare the smoker and cast iron grill. Cousin Luke went for the moon shine. If Auntie Anne found out about it, heads would roll. Cousin Rain Man was the DJ for the party. Aunt Renee prepared the crate of collard greens, Lyan (pounded yam), Dodo (Fried Plantains), and Efo (vegetable soup). Cousin Marvin fried the best chicken in Baltimore. Cousin Marvin's Grandma Ruby prepared the baked macaroni and cheese which contained six different cheeses blended in such a way that a person without teeth will not worry about chewing because it just melts in your mouth. The rest of the family did their share of cooking, but the highlight of the day was Grandma Dottie's deviled eggs. Uncle Butch's grilling techniques could compete with any professional griller. The music at the party consisted of the Nigerian selections, gospel favorites, old school R&B, line dancing, including the electron slide and Chicago Steppin'.

Alex was excited as he prepared for his graduation party. He cleaned the house with exceptional care the day of the party. He felt pressure like a hand of "a grown man's approval" pat him on the back as he finished his chores with a grateful heart. People were on their way and the hand of "approval" was back. Alex smiled because he knew he was going in the right direction with his life.

Auntie Anne's house was set in the middle of a very busy tree-lined neighborhood, located in the section of Baltimore City where homes surrounded by one quarter of an acre of grass and familiar sounds of hard working people are the norm. The neighborhood association prevented the entrance of slum property owners. All property owners in Auntie's neighborhood have legitimate intent. *What a nice neighborhood. I am going to miss it,* Alex thought as he swept the front porch.

The excitement of the graduation party spread with the aroma of the pit roasting lamb, which was a 12-hour undertaking, and the sound of the DJ spinning practice tunes on the turn tables. Excited about seeing some of his Aunties and their children, Alex just wanted to get past the "oh, he's so handsome," "Just a delicious slice of chocolate cake," "You're a heart-breaker," comments his Aunties made every time they greeted him. Alex does enjoy hearing the dialect associated with his mother's native Nigerian tongue. The dialect of his aunties reminded him of his mother. Hearing the aunties engage in conversation caused an ache in Alex's heart that reminded him how much he missed both of his parents while abiding in this land of new beginnings.

Free Will enjoyed the style of Alex's pronunciation. He gives words a British accentuated American executed hip hop flavor vibe that intrigues people to pay attention to the melodies of his dialog. Appointed by Free Will to MC her on-stage performances, Alex began a new focus in life as poetry in motion. Free Will used audiences to give Alex confidence to stand before people and succeed.

Reflecting back, Alex realized that it was the worst mistake of his life that brought him to the land of promise, the place of peace, a deep yearning to listen to the call of God in his spirit that calmed Alex in the midst of trouble. Alex realized that God called him to make an impact on the world. With every epiphany, Drama comes along to dull the enlightenment.

Alex worries that Free Will's best friend, Kasha, who keeps trying to push up on him, will come to the party. He does not understand why someone as forthright as Free Will would hang around someone as wild as she. To make matters worse, Kasha is a good friend of Ten. Ten's real name is Nancy, but she calls herself Ten because her antics on the strip pole are rated a perfect ten by all of her clients. Kasha and Ten, when combined, make up a toxic mix named Trouble. Always touching and feeling on Alex, offering opportunities for entertainment that would not make Free Will proud, Kasha and Ten tempt Alex to compromise an unspoken understanding that he has with his cousin—her friends are off limits. Let us not get it wrong, Alex is not a saint by any stretch of the imagination, but he does not want to do anything that would compromise his relationship with Free Will or Auntie Anne.

Trying to keep the terrible duo of Kasha and Ten off his

mind, Alex reflected back on how his parents fought to have a relationship in spite of the opposition they faced. It is in his parents' fight to be and stay together that gives Alex the strength to see the light in the middle of the dark tunnel he entered several years ago. It is a story of love, heartbreak, and resurrection into the endearment of God's love where Alex will complete his rehabilitation and American education. He prepared to go back home to take his rightful seat beside his father when the time is right.

Life in America has provided Alex a new level of healing powered by purpose to look ahead and not behind at past mistakes. Embracing Philippians 3:14, Alex repeats in prayer "I will press toward the mark of the prize of the high calling of God in Christ Jesus." With suitcase in hand, purpose chiseled in his heart and desire to fulfill his dream in America, Alex proceeded with a smile towards his destination—the Boston College campus. A heartfelt hug and warm kiss on the cheek of Auntie Anne and Free Will, Alex would never be the same again because he revealed the secret of his pain to Free Will the night before. With the secret released, he went on his way to find peace.

*****

Alex went off to college and seldom came back to his cousin Free Will's neighborhood to stay with either she or Auntie Anne. Instead, he stayed in Boston, regained his love for life, and put behind him the troubles experienced at home in London. Alex stopped using his American accent, healed his mind, body, and spirit as the President of the student body, and excelled as part of the rowing team. Alex was becoming more and more comfortable in his desire to reconcile with his father.

CHAPTER TEN

The Teacher searched to find just the right words, and what he wrote was upright and true.
Ecclesiastes 12:10 (NIV)

Brock in College

BROCK'S EXCEPTIONAL ACADEMIC ABILITY ALLOWED him to carry a heavy course load each semester and during the summer placed him ahead of his entering classmates. The short period he and Angel had together on campus was very important to Angel. Her big brother was everything to her. Every minute with him was like a day of sunshine. Angel entered college two years after Brock, but three years behind because his accelerated pursuit of credits allowed him to be ranked as a senior.

Extremely proud of Brock's accomplishments, Mom Johnson, Angel, and Poppa wagged their tongues positively about him every chance life supplied. Bragging about Brock became a competitive sport run by three world class promoters: Mom Johnson, Angel, and Poppa. Brock ingested their compliments that resulted in no waste; it gave off energy to productively burn the midnight oil. His energy reserves were stored in advance for the grueling days that awaited this budding medical intern.

Brock had many late night telephone conversations with Poppa; it was man talk not shared with women. Poppa encouraged Brock to pray and to begin a serious spiritual walk. Angel was right beside him. They both were very comfortable about spreading the gospel in action and deed. Delighted to have his little sister with him, Brock enjoyed watching over her. Attending church with his little sister equated to the picture perfect sibling relationship visualized in Brock's mind. Angel joined the gospel choir at college with the intent of expounding upon her extraordinary vocal abilities. Brock went to as many gospel choir events as his schedule would allow. Pew buddies is how they refer to themselves as they invite friends and dorm mates to attend church with them.

Collaborative siblings going through the college experience together, Brock was determined not to expose Angel to his former relationship with DRAMA. Shielding Angel from anyone or any circumstance that did not uplift her, like some members of the track team, Angel was an important part of Brock's family unit that had his best intentions foremost in their minds.

Angel was used to Brock having a lot of women chasing after him trying to get his attention. It was a secret passion of Angel to watch Brock watch Free Will whenever she performed at the campus café on Friday nights. Always traveling the country, Free Will spit her rhymes on college campuses to keep the vibe based in reality. Free Will is the first young woman Angel witnessed Brock watch with positive moral intent. In other words, it appeared that Brock was interested in getting to know Free Will as a person, friend, and confidant prior to leaping into a serious girl-friend boy-friend relationship. This was evident to Angel because Brock always wanted to talk about the poetic lyrics of Free Will and not talk about her physical attributes in the way he did with the other women on campus. Getting the attention of Free Will was Brock's prayer and Angel knew it.

In the past, if Brock thought some "babe was giving him the eye," he would savor that kind of attention. There was something different about Free Will. She fell outside of the "babe" category. That was different for Brock—scary to him when he reflected on his behavior towards Free Will. It was not about him anymore, it was all about her. Now that Angel was on campus with Brock, she made up her mind that it was her job to make the Brock-Free Will connection.

Two years had passed since Alex's graduation party where Angel first noticed the secret glances. At that time, Angel dropped hints to Free Will about how, "Brock is a really good guy who would make the right girl a nice boy-friend." Free Will did not take the bait. She did not appear to have any interest in getting to know Brock. She in turn spoke highly about Alex. Angel thought to herself, *I don't know Alex nor do I want to know him for that matter.* Turning the table a little bit, Free Will pulled out pictures of Alex and encouraged Angel to get to know him. Angel did not bite; as a sophomore in high school, she thought a graduating high school senior was out of her league. Angel enjoyed the graduation party and continued to scheme new ways to drop more hints about Brock to her play cousin, Free Will.

*****

During Brock's first year in college, Angel had permission from her Mom coupled with encouragement from Poppa to hang out on campus with her big brother, Brock. Angel stayed in the freshman female dorm with one of Brock's taste of honey. The evening before the event, Angel dressed early and promenaded to the student lounge to chill, awaiting Brock's entrance. The orchestrated interlude in the shower exulted in the excellence of a brother that was just fresh, clean, and in control, as the old folks say, cool. Angel's proud little sister demeanor sat under the shadow of Brock's coolness to anoint her the same.

In preparation of the evening's event, Angel thought of a way to make the Brock-Free Will connection as she saw Free Will's cousin, Alex, in the distance. She thought, *What a Geek.* Flocked with the curly black hair and black rim glasses, and wearing clothes that did not make any statement of fashion whatsoever, Alex did not seem as distant as he appeared at his high school graduation party. Completely startled by her sudden presence, Alex moved back when he realized Angel had entered his private zone.

Angel, on a mission to find out the 411 regarding Free Will's dating status, overlooked his appearance and focused on her mission to find answers. Angel wanted to know if Free Will had a boyfriend or a special someone. Understanding that not all cousins hang out together or have privy to that kind of information, Angel was willing to prod Alex's brain for information about Free Will. Alex was not shy about explaining how important Free Will was to him. Their relationship is deep for reasons that only God can explain. Alex was not prepared to tell Angel the graphic personal details of his life. For Angel, the conversation was over; he did not help at all. Without a salutation, Angel walked away. Angel did not know how to take Alex, but his politeness and willingness to engage in conversation was intimidating. Angel thought, *Too bad, the path for his life took him to an entirely different college, in an entirely different state. He is out of my league anyway.*

Angel's departure provoked Alex into deep thought, *I was an addict. I am glad my parents decided Free Will would be the kind of role model who would guide me down the road to recovery. Free Will is the best. I will not introduce her to anyone who may cause her heartache. I witnessed*

Brock break a lot of hearts when we were on the high school team together. Free Will would not be one of Brock's conquests if I have anything to do with it. Brock appeared in the lounge immediately after Alex left. He and Angel ventured into the campus café. Alex watched them from a distance.

Brock was completely spellbound by the poet, Free Will, who was there for a weekend engagement. Brock had a major crush on her. He was completely unaware of Angel's effort to make the Brock-Free Will connection. Rome, Brock's confidant, was aware of every angle of the non-interlocking Brock-Free Will connection. Telling a close friend about his crush or sharing any personal feelings was new for Brock, but Rome was his boy. Prior to his "college boy" days, Brock did not share his private thoughts with anyone. He attempted to open up to the fact that real brothers can be trusted. There is honor associated with being part of a brotherhood that allows one to share their deepest secrets. Rome was part of that special club.

The poets at the evening's event on the campus café spit rhymes in front of enthusiastic audiences. Brock was completely fascinated with Free Will. He felt Free Will's poetic flow spit over the audience so much so that those in love with her purpose, like he, desired not to use an umbrella so the spit would be fully felt. Not all appreciated Free Will, like he. The joy of her abundant perfectly adorned flesh, granted appropriateness to a dream that manifested into nightly pubescent physical attributes. In other words, Free Will gave a young man happy dreams. Fascinated by the two hundred plus pound beauty that stood on a 5'4" frame, Brock imagined adorning her in the most precious attire; presenting her to the world as his queen. Free Will, a poet's poet who deserved a man's man; Brock wanted to be that man.

Brock sat in the café witnessing the performances. He thought back to the first time he saw Free Will. It was at Alex's high school graduation party. He was afraid then, and was still afraid to speak to her. Brock thought, "I don't have any problems attracting females. They notice me and most girls will do just about anything to get my attention. I have had my share of experiences with Kasha, Ten, Tracey, Amber, Molly and more. There is something special about Free Will that makes me want to break the code." The exertion required to break the code was new for Brock.

Captivated by the excellent poets, Angel wrapped her mind around Free Will's ministry disguised as a performance. Angel caught a glimpse of what it may be like to develop God's given gift of singing. Singing is a spiritual gift that rests in the center of God's peace. Angel knew by witnessing the peace of God on Free Will's face, His power flows through her words. The desire to perform publicly was beginning to rise in Angel.

*****

Rome knew that Brock felt comfortable being around the track team members collectively. Brock was beginning to open up about his thoughts, feelings and aspirations. There was a special bond between the four by one hundred meter relay team. Brock felt strong in Rome's circle of friends. The circle of friends dealt with small things, hanging out, just chillin', chasing women on campus, and more, but the circle of friendship would never violate the confidence of a fellow friend.

The protection of confidence was very important for Brock because in his home life prior to becoming a member of the Johnson family he lived and died by deceit. Deceitfulness was a way of life. Brock's birth family would deceive the law, the landlord, public officials trying to pen down their tax status and more. His relay team brothers represented truth, not deception and lies. Rome, however, made a choice to yield to the sin nature and sought to betray Brock's confidence in the area of personal relationships.

The truth about the lie Rome lived is the fact that he is envious of Brock's ability to attract women without any effort. Women adore Brock in spite of his inability to afford the finer things in life. They find something pleasing about Brock, which makes them want to spend time with him. The women do not care that he does not have a stable birth family that he would want to take anyone home to meet. Rome has a secret axe to grind with Brock. Rome is still secretly fuming over his inability to attract Reba. He worked his best rap from the "Get the girl for life" playbook but was heartbroken when all Brock did was come into the room and Reba had eyes only for Brock. Rome completely overlooked the fact that Brock did not give the girl an opportunity to do anything more than to say "Hello" and did not give her a second thought. Unbeknownst to Brock, Rome had it out for Brock from that point forward.

The truth of the matter is, Reba could see straight through Rome's great smile into his lustful intentions. His intentions made Reba feel like Rome was looking for a freak—not a girlfriend. That was her clue to move her focus elsewhere. Just then, Brock came through the door. Brock was different. Reba did not need or desire the lustful glares of a man because she gets plenty of male attention at home from her six brothers and step-father. Reba appreciated the fact that Brock did not look at her lustfully. She wanted to get to know him more. Unfortunately, for Reba,

Brock did not want to continue their conversation beyond "hello." That did not stop Rome from seeking revenge against Brock. Reba continued to be nice, but kept her distance from Rome. She really wanted to get to know Brock beyond the basic friendship level. It was her desire that Brock would ask her out; it was not going to happen. Rome continued to try to fill the category above friendship level. Reba had an excuse to brush Rome off repeatedly. Finally, Rome saw Reba on campus and just asked her straight, "What is wrong with me? Why won't you go out with me?" Reba said, "There is nothing wrong with you, Rome, I am just interested in a different type of guy." Rome replied, "I saw how you looked a Brock." Reba responded, "If you noticed, he never looked back at me the same way. Let it go, Rome, and I have let it go that I will never go out with Brock; your boy would never step on your heart. Trust me, I tried everything—he will not betray you." Brock would not even allow Reba to stay in the friend category because he could see the impact on Rome. Brock cut off all communication with Reba—not even "Hello." Rome was his family. Brock was not about to let anyone or anything destroy his family unit.

Rome did not see it that way. Rome secretly saw Brock as a "Blocker." In Rome's mind, the only way to stop a blocker is sweet revenge. Rome was out for revenge that Brock had not geared up to protect himself for. Rome was living the lie entitled "Best-Friend/Brother." From Brock's perspective, there was no reason for him to believe the term "Best-Friend/Brother" was a lie that did not reflect the experiences of their day-to-day relationship. Rome's one-sided revenge was about to destroy the track-team family unit Brock wanted to call his own.

CHAPTER ELEVEN

"Obey them not only to win their favor when their eye is on you, but like slaves of Christ, doing the will of God from your heart"
Ephesians 6:6 (NIV)

Aubrey & Amara's Story

A T AGE TEN, ALEX'S MOTHER, Amara, arrived in London after being awarded a private scholarship to the Elite Royal Academy of London. The boarding school sprawled across a beautifully manicured campus that housed regal buildings embracing the historical stories of world-wide royalty. Radiant, pleasant, confident, humble, beautiful, distant, protected, and guarded were terms that described Amara. She was not part of the social elite class because of her humble beginnings; snobbish students viewed Amara as part of the social underclass.

The social elite were very different from Amara, and they knew not to mumble a simple negative word nor offer a repulsive gaze in her direction. There was something different about Amara that let onlookers know not to anger God by blaspheming her name. As a result of the clique's inability to penetrate her ordained wall of protection, Amara walked in solidarity with the spirit of excellence God had given her. Amara's light positively hid in the shadow of her unapproachable radius.

Students who controlled the entrance to the courtyard represented third generation celebrity children—all of whom wore the formal title of royalty or the social elite. The students who befriended Amara invited her home for the holidays. Though friendly, the students could not get past Amara's wall that protected her behind deeply set black eyes.

Warm in their appearance, Amara's eyes said to onlookers, "You can look, but don't touch." It was the intentional stares of one student in particular who caught Amara's attention. That individual was the son of King Winston Buckington who was only allowed to court individuals of royal heritage. Amara knew where the line between the social classes was drawn and had no desire to cross the line.

With a long line of family roots and the path to matrimony rolled out in the form of a red carpet, Prince Aubrey Buckington was heir to the throne. At 6'4", Aubrey was a cricket, rugby and equestrian champion. The list of female suitors along with family arranged meetings was both exciting and exhausting for Aubrey. He was beginning to grow tired of young women who dared not show him their true selves in an attempt to win his heart. He wanted the challenge of being involved with an independent soul, a self-starter, a woman with a purpose. Dressed with a new set of eyes, Aubrey scanned the campus of young women at the academy looking for a chance to meet his match.

High school graduation day was fast approaching. The same group of young women with the same personalities were growing equally weary to Aubrey at an equal pace. Aubrey had a family history, a heritage, a social order to maintain, yet he could not keep Amara out of his mind. He learned of Amara's name when his tasteless friends discussed what they would love to do sexually with the beautiful Nigerian native. Fuming from within, Aubrey abruptly left the group at that time and later kicked himself for not speaking up against the shameful talk. Aubrey knew he needed to contain himself because it was only two weeks earlier when he would have led the discussion like that, now he had a change of heart.

Aubrey dreamt about the possibility of meeting the African beauty name Amara. He heard other friends speak about her exceptional intelligence, her God-centered lifestyle and an inability to participate in youthful foolishness due to her God-ordained assignment. It was not in the derogatory way that Aubrey was interested in meeting her, it was his desire that Amara somehow was included on the list of possible acceptable suitors. He wished, prayed and hope for a chance to meet her.

Amara was a 5'10", beautiful coco colored skin that adorned a size ten frame that popular diet companies would not dare to approach because it did not contain an ounce of excess fat. Being in complete agreement with her mood motivated her style for the day. The length of Amara's natural dark brown micro braids reached the center of her back glistening with the free flowing style that acquiesce the mood of her morning. Amara knew how to cover herself nicely. Her rhythmic pace made by her footsteps reflected her graceful walk. Amara commanded respect as she moved about the room in a positive awe. Only "Haters" did not appreciate her energy.

Amara felt Aubrey's stares. She felt his change in heart. Amara attributed the change to God's presence in his life, the power of prayer and God's ability to answer any prayer. Confident about whom she was and going to become in the world, and what she had to bring to a relationship motivated Amara to pen heartfelt expressions to Aubrey.

There were two days remaining before graduation day. There was a slight question in the mind of Aubrey regarding his ability to rise to the occasion set before him. Could he gather his nerves so that he could meet the girl of his dreams before everyone departed to attend college? Could Aubrey say, "Good

Morning" to Amara? With only two days remaining, the clock was ticking—their heartbeats were in sync. Nothing. Amara was nowhere in sight. Was the dream over? One day remained. Would Amara come to her normal spot to hang out? Would she stay in the dorm because all of her final exams were finished? Only God could make this dream a reality.

In the Academy's dining room, Aubrey looked for signs of Amara. It happened. God had answered his prayers. Across the room, Aubrey was excited to witness Amara come to eat breakfast. Aubrey got up to meet her as she entered the room only to be intercepted by Abigail who had been waiting for the chance to give her last pitch to win Aubrey over. Maintaining the posture of a gentleman, Aubrey gave Abigail his attention. While standing there with a fake smile and wondering thoughts, Aubrey felt saddened by the missed opportunity to meet Amara. Aubrey only heard "bah, bah, bah, bah" coming out of Abigail's mouth—not realizing he agreed to meet her for tea after the evening's cricket match. The phrase "It is over," repeated in Aubrey's mind like a broken record. The last chance to meet Amara was defunct because of Abigail. *So what if she is the daughter of the Russian Prime Minister, I am not interested*, Aubrey thought. On the other hand, Abigail felt like she had won the prize; a date with the prince—the heir to the throne.

It was graduation day at the Royal Academy of London. Excitement was in the air. The chatter of family members coupled with the chance to meet celebrities in person made the occasion exceptional for the body of students there on scholarship. The tickets to the graduation were hotter than a ticket to the local rock and roll concert. Aubrey was anxious about the possibility of stepping outside of his comfort zone to meet the beautiful Amara. How different it was for him not to seek the attention of a female classmate but to become the pursuer. It was his last opportunity to meet Amara, the "one" who made his heart flutter and stomach churn in a wonderful way. Today was the day.

On the third day, Jesus rose from the tomb. *Could the third day be the time he could rise to the occasion and meet Amara,* Aubrey thought. The sky was perfect. The sun beamed with warmth intertwined with excitement. The rays of light touched Amara's cheeks. Aubrey practiced in his mind again and again the words, "Good Day." That is how he would greet her. Aubrey thought, I will say, "Good Day" with a smile. "It is so nice to meet you. I hope we can correspond as we both leave here to attend college." What a great opening conversation, Aubrey thought.

To the surprise of Aubrey, Amara was second in the graduating class, which meant she was to sit next to him on the graduation stage. With thanks given to God upon learning the news, Aubrey readied himself to take his place on the stage. Unbeknownst to him, there was a surprise guest for the graduation. The guest who was to sit next to him was not Amara. Amara was moved to sit in the first row on the floor with the graduation class.

An overwhelming applause for the surprise guest, Aubrey's father, King Winston Buckington did not ease the tension in Aubrey's spirit. Everyone in the room was elated to sit in the audience of the king. Although, it was comforting for Aubrey to see his father again, Aubrey's nerves got worse when his father arrived. First, he knew his father would never approve Amara as an acceptable girlfriend because of her heritage and lack of royal upbringing. Second, Aubrey's father would monopolize all Aubrey's time, which would eliminate Aubrey's chance to speak with Amara before she moved away forever.

Amara's stately posture belied her poor upbringing. She was a walking contradiction of how someone can represent stately eloquence in the face of poverty. Her grace attracted Aubrey in spite of her background. All hope of meeting Amara vanished from Aubrey's mind in the face of the change in the graduation program.

In spite of everything that happened, the graduation program went well for Aubrey. All were pleased to hear his speech. Aubrey's father smiled as if he was personally involved with the preparation of the speech. The graduation and associated ceremonies had concluded. All the hugs were given. Every handshake passed the test. It was time to move on. The bags were packed and the car was waiting in the front. No more good-byes. No more waves. No more glances. The slow unfulfilled walk toward the car in front ensued. Everyone left the room, the driver opened the door in time with Aubrey's forward motion. "Thank you," he said to the chauffeur. As he turned to close the car door, Amara appeared. Trapped by his arm and the bend of the car door she smiled and said, "Good luck to you, Aubrey." With a quick hug and light kiss on the cheek, Amara disappeared as quickly as she appeared. Still in shock by the unlikeliness of the scenario that just occurred, Aubrey felt his vest pocket only to find an envelope that contained a handwritten note.

CHAPTER TWELVE

An Answered Prayer

"So we fasted and petitioned our God about this, and he answered our prayer."
Ezra 8:23 (NIV)

Amara's Letter to Aubrey

It is my prayer before I leave the royal academy forever that God gives me the chance to become acquainted with you, Aubrey. It is within the will of God I prayed we would meet. Since you are reading this letter, the meeting has occurred.

Please let me take this opportunity to introduce myself. My name is Amara Rachel Oni. I have been at the Royal Academy of London on a full academic scholarship. A very nice Christian graciously paid my tuition for this magnificent school. In front of my life is a full scholarship to Oxford University and a chance to reside in America with my Christian sponsor upon graduation. It is my desire to succeed in life, make my family proud and after graduation from college, I will ultimately meet a God-fearing man that may someday become my husband.

Graduating second in my class surpassed my dream to graduate in the top 10 percent. What is most exciting about my graduation is ranking directly behind the number one graduate—you. Your academic prowess and effortless approach to study had many people, like myself, marveling at your brilliance.

This letter is an extension of my faith that we may someday meet. The caring compassion in your eyes touched my heart. As a result, I prayed that God would give me the backbone to write this letter. Some may think this letter too bold for a Christian woman to write. I also think it could be determined as it could be a reflection of loose principles, none of which is true. Writing this letter steps me outside of my comfort zone and places my trust in God that you have grown into a young man saved by grace waiting for God to give you a sign of His existence.

I know that many people email to stay in contact, but I desire that you receive this hand written note as an opportunity to experience who I am by what I have done with my hands. I believe from my heart to your heart, God directly whispers in the ear of the recipient. Please before you continue reading, meditate to hear God speak directly to you.

MEDITATION MOMENT

If you hear God confirm in your spirit all that I have said thus far, and you believe it is in the plan of God we stay in contact with one another, please use the address specified on the envelop to correspond if you so desire. Aubrey, may God continue to watch over you. We both know "…that in all things God works for the good of those who love him, who have been called according to his purpose." (Romans 8:28).

Sincerely,

Amara Rachel Oni

CHAPTER THIRTEEN

This is what the LORD says: "In the time of my favor I will answer you, and in the day of salvation I will help you; I will keep you and will make you to be a covenant for the people, to restore the land and to reassign its desolate inheritances."
Isaiah 49:8 (NIV)

Aubrey

THE EARTH STOPPED AFTER AUBREY finished reading Amara's letter. "Did she say, 'The caring compassion in your eyes touched my heart?' I cannot believe it." Beads of sweat rolled down Aubrey's face as he pondered the possibility of corresponding with his Dream—Amara. Compared to all the riches in his family, none matched the value of her smile. On a cloud, Aubrey's feet seem to rest two inches above the ground as he walked from the car into the hotel that evening.

Nestled in the chair looking out of the window thinking about what he was going to say to Amara, the telephone rang. Still on the cloud, Aubrey picked up the telephone—it was the front desk. Abigail was at the desk and requested permission to come into the suite to speak with Aubrey. Not giving the request any thought, he authorized her admittance to his Royal suite intending on greeting her kindly and getting back to his letter writing as soon as she departed.

Abigail entered the royal suite and greeted Aubrey with the traditional kiss on each cheek, a warm hug and a smile. She felt slightly betrayed because Aubrey agreed to meet her for tea after his cricket match but left with his friends without acknowledging her presence. She started the conversation by saying, "I missed having tea with you after the cricket match several days ago." Aubrey said, "I apologize—I had a meeting with my father after the match." He did not realize that he had agreed to the outing during the occasion when she cornered him into a conversation. "All is well," said Abigail. Aubrey finally realized that Abigail's intentions crossed the line of a social visit—she was looking for action as suggested by the tight fitting dress and seductive stare.

Aubrey was not the same person he was the night they first met. In the past, he was looking for a hot sweaty night that could only be spoken about in a room filled with young men. He had changed. Aubrey wanted a real relationship. Abigail did not fit the bill for a real relationship. Aubrey spoke in a mature concerned tone and said, "Wait a minute, Abigail. If I in any way implied that my interest in you goes beyond causal friendship, please forgive me." In response, Abigail was not deterred when she said, "Don't worry, after what I am about to put on you, I know you will feel differently." Backing away from Abigail, Aubrey put his hand in his pocket, grabbed the controller to press the first button. The room telephone immediately started ringing. Picking up the telephone to greet an imaginary caller was a trick the Royal family used to excuse themselves out of the conversation in the room. Aubrey was smooth in his conversation with the pretend caller. He covered the phone and asked Abigail if she could show herself out as he took the call.

Not happy at the manner in which she was asked to leave, Abigail put on her coat and left the room in a huff. The elevator from the penthouse was private and those without a key could only get off and on at the ground level. Always prepared to save face regardless of the outcome, Abigail saw Amara in the elevator lobby prepared to visit her Christian sponsor. "Why are you here?" Abigail barked at Amara. Amara ignored the tone and replied, "I am going to see my sponsor—the person who so graciously agreed to pay for my college tuition, room and board."

As Amara got onto the elevator and the doors were about to close, Abigail said, "I hope you have more luck than I did." Not quite understanding the meaning behind the statement, Amara smiled and said to the porter as the door closed, "Penthouse, please." In one of the five bedrooms in the suite, Aubrey's father was resting, but knew that the student he sponsored would be coming by for a visit. Excited to meet such an outstanding student who represents what education could do to get people out of a poor background, he wanted his son to feel inspiration by such a person as she.

Once in the suite, she was escorted to the sitting room. Amara was the picture of beauty. She practiced her introduction again and again. King Winston Buckington entered the room and Aubrey reluctantly followed. Upon entering the room, Amara stood to her feet to shake the hand of the King and from around the corner she saw Aubrey. She opened her mouth to speak, but the only thing that came out was air. For the first time in Amara's life, she was completely speechless as was Aubrey. The connection that was made with Amara's letter, confirmed as "accepted" based on the approving expression on Aubrey's face.

After the formal meeting with the King ended, Aubrey was very happy to sit and get to know a very intelligent woman who could inspire him to see brilliance and not race. The four hour discussion resulted in a commitment to begin a friendship. Before they went their separate ways to college, they met each day for the two weeks remaining. The conversations centered on the topics of world peace, purpose, God, and love.

Aubrey and Amara fell in love and each wore as a gesture of a promise, a ring Aubrey had as part of a collection given to him by his grandmother. This promise ring would be worn by each until the relationship resolved itself or evolved into holy matrimony.

Upon college graduation, Aubrey sought and received permission to marry Amara. They had five sons. Alexander, the eldest son was destined to break the family curse. Amara, against the wishes of the royal family, prepared Alexander for his midnight departure to live in the United States of America with her eldest sister. Anne would take on the job of offering a place of restoration, regain his confidence and purpose under the guidance of his cousin, Free Will.

CHAPTER FOURTEEN

The Rice in Your Puddin'

*"When wisdom entereth into thine heart, and knowledge is pleasant
unto thy soul; Discretion shall preserve thee, understanding shall
keep thee…"*
Proverbs 2:10-11 (KJV)

Brother Michael

BROCK AND HIS TEAM MATES stopped attending the campus chapel and started attending a local church because the church staff fed college students a home cooked meal on Sunday evening. The "Big Mama in the Kitchen" cooked southern baked chicken with candied yams and green beans every week. It was worth the trip. In the process of anticipating the meal, the team listened to the preacher who started ministering to their life's situation. It was as if the preacher witnessed their life experiences before entering the church building and gave them solutions to their problems. The meal was good, but Brock really looked forward to the dynamic pastor who preached real good sermons every Sunday.

One great thing about the weekly church visit, was meeting Brother Michael. Brother Michael had moved south to complete law school and his Master of Theology concurrently. He had taken Brock under his wing. Dallas Davis, his former Armor bearer, was part of a collegiate of males in the rites of passage program in his former church. Brother Michael saw something special in Brock that required additional time to nurture his obvious gifts. Brock was not aware of his gift to bring peace to a chaotic situation. Although a confident young man, Brock had just as many problems as the rest, but was an overcomer. He could rest in the midst of terrible circumstances and saw a way out. When others only see fog, the silver lining guided Brock to an appropriate solution. When his dorm mates could only see that going to church meant waking up before noon, Brock would proudly talk about God and how the preacher was great, and the Sunday meal was excellent. Brock did not let something like "time" stop him from obtaining his blessing.

It was over a month ago that Brock was out late one night with a group of male friends, just chillin' and the police identified him as a wanted criminal. Without an opportunity to explain who he was or what he was doing, Brock was whisked away in the police cruiser down to central booking for processing. He felt frightened and alone. Brock had only one thought and that was to call the church attorney, Brother Michael. Without hesitation, Brother Michael came to the police station and got Brock out of the mistaken identity situation in less than two hours.

A man of few words, Brother Michael offered Brock a place to rest his head and a warm meal to settle his spirit. An obvious place where peace prevails, Brother Michael's home was welcoming and a nice bachelor pad for a preacher in training. Formally trained to preach, Brother Michael ministered through his lifestyle to many brothers looking for an answer. The answer is having a relationship with Jesus Christ. Brock knew before he entered the home of Brother Michael that the answer to life's problems is Jesus Christ. Michael understood completely that Jesus paid the price so that we may have abundant life. He was a great example for young men. The Word of God rested in Brother Michael's spirit and the joy of the Lord was his strength. It was the knowledge of the goodness of the Lord that enabled Brother Michael to see the good in all people. The gang was still tugging at Brock. To be frank about the matter, Brock liked the tug because it made him feel wanted and loved. The emotional commitment to academic pursuit has allowed Brock to side step gang activity and focus.

The call of God also lingered in the back of Brock's mind. It was God's voice that made him long to be in church every Sunday rather than simply read the Bible alone in the dorm room. Brock was no dummy. He realized that it was the goodness of the Lord and his personal relationship with Jesus Christ that had kept him off the streets away from the gangs. Brock often pondered the relationship between the church and the gang. He thought to himself, *The downside to church life for Brock was the lack of human touch and positive engagement from church elders. Not true with the gang, but the engagement was to do harm which was not good. So there is still a slight tug where doing right can be very lonely and doing wrong can be very engaging. Why isn't doing right engaging as well? Or is it engagement and I have not had the right set of Christians to engage with?* That made church people seem cold to Brock sometimes. Brother Michael was a bright spot at church. He was able to reach the young males with a hand shake and fist bump. He brought positive reinforcement that everything will be all right. Brother Michael helped young men to know that Jesus is real.

Church folk do not always invite you to be part of their activities if you are not on the church "A" list. The "A" list people are those individuals who sit at the head table, receive special invitations from the Pastor, and are not an after thought on the invitation list. Unfortunately, in the gang, all willing participants are on the "A" list. The rules of the invitees are not limited to persons with a pedigree and/or a title. The rule of engagement for the gang is the desire to ride and die.

Brother Michael had a greater pull on Brock than the gangs because he made Brock feel like he was on the "A+" list; that is the type of list Brock was looking to be part of. The most important thing about Brother Michael was he not only made you feel special, he also sticks close until you could walk your own journey down the road with Jesus Christ as your Lord and Savior. It is not about dress code, but about being a part of the "Blessed code," says Brother Michael. The recipe for any good rice pudding requires rice. The recipe for the life as a Christian requires having a relationship with the Lord and Savior, Jesus Christ. Brother Michael taught the love of Jesus by demonstrating love. Brother Michael helped young men appreciate the rice in the pudding.

CHAPTER FIFTEEN

The Evil Behind the Smile

"The face of the LORD is against those who do evil, to cut off the memory of them from the earth."
Psalm 34:16 (NIV)

Commencement

ROME'S ACCEPTANCE INTO SEVERAL LAW schools provided something to look forward to in the future. After weeks of pondering his prospects, he selected Harvard Law as his program of choice. Randall, the third member of their high school track team, elected to stay at their current college, obtain a graduate degree in education, and become an assistant coach for the track team. Brock received acceptance from several medical schools. He actively contemplated which school best supported his desired outcome. As a college graduation gift for all of them, Brother Michael had the church sponsor their trip to the international singles' conference.

Angel was excited that they elected to accept the invitation offered to attend the conference because she was on the schedule to sing at the conference's Thursday and Friday Night young adult poetry explosion. It is traditional at the conference, that the best young Christian talent showcase their gifts in the mix and mingle setting.

International Singles' Conference

EVERYONE AT THE SINGLES' CONFERENCE WENT to the poetry exposition that started at 1:00 a.m. The Master of Ceremony came to the stage to introduce the first talent. When Free Will came to the stage as the opening act, Brock looked over to Angel and she just smiled back. Butterflies journeyed through his stomach and up his back. Brock was so excited that he could not sit still. Brock continually followed Free Will with his heart. Over the years, she started to notice him in the neighborhood or in the audience supporting Angel. Brock still could not approach Free Will because he did not want to disturb his family unit provided by his boys on the track team. Rome was interested in Free Will, which made her off-limits to Brock.

With a smile that was very attractive to the women, Rome can pull any woman. Brock felt like he could not compete with all that Rome had to offer a woman, so he elected not to pursue Free Will. He could only watch from a distance. Angel could see right through Brock's mask and prayed he would have the desire to follow his heart in a manner that did not disturb his idea of a family unit.

Rome showed up at the poetry explosion putting out nonverbal expressions of interest toward Free Will. She had gone through this many times in her life, where a very active young man may show interest, but because he is too insecure to let his friends know he is interested in a plus size person, he would only approach Free Will under the cover of night or the disguise of "Just Friends." For lack of a better term, Free Will labels this behavior, evil. People are evil to her if they knowingly hide their true feelings, especially if the intent is to deceive others. She is not quite sure, but Rome looks like he may be a deceiver. If that is true, Free Will can only see him as evil just like the others. More importantly, the person she is interested in having a friendship with does not speak to her at all.

Rome is a very charming and handsome young man. His charm did not work with Free Will because she saw straight through his lying eyes and bright smile. The evil behind Rome's smile snapped her attention out of this deceptive grip. Free Will was seeking God's choice to date a man who loved the Lord and wanted to do right by her—Brock, the man she does not know personally. Angel has introduced him to Free Will during their many conversations. When Brock looks into Free Will's eyes when she is on stage, he experiences her lyrical intent intertwined in his prayer for the chance to meet her. After completing the lyrical session of her life at the singles' conference, Free Will emotionally removed herself from Rome's evil intent. God's glory covered her session of rhymes that provoked thoughts of the goodness of the Lord in the midst of life's struggles. Rings from the snapping of fingers, in concert with positive head nodding, pushed the spirit throughout the room in the freshness of young adults awakening with God. Free Will felt as if all in the room felt her zone.

Summoned to Rome's table, Free Will was not interested, but went anyway. Immediately upon sitting at Rome's table, Free

Will witnessed him slip his number on the bill for the server to retrieve. She did not need to wonder anymore. The behavior behind his smile did not respect her space enough to wait and exchange numbers after she had left the area. What a wonderful confirmation God delivered right in the middle of the spoken word session. God also allowed Free Will to see the evil behind the smile. God's purpose was known and real for the season where discernment was important.

Free Will's cousin, Alex, who also graduated from college, came to the conference as a farewell before he left to go home to London to reconcile with his family. Alex could see how the cherubim placed peace in Free Will's face. There was focus of "what's next" in her smile. The popcorn goodness of her smile felt like a good thing to witness. Free Will was happy with how God stepped into her life to show-up and show-out and place her on the path of "purpose."

Alex looked sadly relieved. It was difficult for Free Will to figure out what was going on with her cousin. Alex said, "I received a letter from my father for my twenty-fourth birthday. I knew he would not forget my birthday, but I never thought he would provide a written apology." Alex cried as he said, "My mother sent me here to America to break the curse of abuse that has been in both my parents' families for many years. I hated the beatings, but importantly, I hated leaving my family because my father would not stop physically abusing me. He wants me home. The curse is broken." The crying continued as Free Will wrapped her arms around her cousin so he could complete his uncontrollable crying. She whispered in his ear, "Baby boy, it is finished. It is time to go home. I thank God for His healing power."

CHAPTER SIXTEEN

The Apology

"To give his people the knowledge of salvation
through the forgiveness of their sins,"
Luke 1:77 (NIV)

Dearest Alexander...

Dearest Alexander,

I am so proud that your wall has a degree in International Finance hanging to greet onlookers. Your mark in the world represented by your degree is a sign of better times ahead. Focus on that which is in front of you and do not grow bitter and angry like me. Your God-given gift to communicate will provide good cheer and merriment to all who will meet you; what a blessing. I am proud of the man you have become.

As a child, you had the ability to know someone's gift by simply looking into his or her eyes. It is most unfortunate that I once tried everything in my power to break your spirit. Determined to deter your confidence, your mother was wise to ship you off to America to start a new life. Her insight to put you in a safe environment was the best decision to allow both of us to heal.

I thank you for never representing me publicly as the "jerk" who thought it his right to physically abuse you. Now my life has changed by my new walk with Christ. As a blood washed born again believer in Jesus Christ, I seek your forgiveness. You had many chances to tell the world how terrible I was, but you never revealed your difficult home life. As a changed man, I look forward to the day when we will meet face-to-face in celebration of your return.

Please do whatever you must to protect your children from abusive people. Uplift your family. Look to God for inspiration. Do not miss the inspiration right in front of you. Do not get distracted by surface beauties with no direction or purpose in life. Remember, if you keep pace with God, you will not run into a wall that He has already padded for your impact. Stay true to who God designed you to be.

I miss being the father you deserve. Rather than supporting you, it was all about me. I was so wrong. I am sorry. I apologize. I love you. Please forgive me.

Come home and take your rightful seat next to me.

Eternally grateful,

Your Papa,
(John 3:16)

CHAPTER SEVENTEEN

Thank You Opens the Door to... You're Welcome

"As you enter the home, give it your greeting."
Matthew 10:12 (NIV)

Brock

THE SENIOR YEAR OF COLLEGE is now part of the rear view mirror in time. Brock is on his way to medical school. The notches on his belt symbolize his female conquests. He visited the candy shop of female delights on campus on many occasions but his heart's desire is Free Will. Angel, now entering her junior year in college is happy many of her friends attended the annual singles' conference as an act of consecration before they graduated and entered the next level of education.

Brock decided that after receiving acceptance into several medical schools he needed to clear his head before making his decision as to where he should go. There were several schools interested in him, but his heart was with Howard University School of Medicine. Following his heart was very important for Brock. So many voices continue to give their opinion about what is best for him. All Brock wanted to do is clear his head to make space for God to speak. The annual singles' conference helped him to seek God for clarity for his future endeavor.

The theme of this year's conference was: *"Achieving Oneness With God."* Brock's prayer was to allow God to bring forth healing power in his life. He wanted healing from the fear of rejection, abandonment, and entering into a meaningful relationship. Brock did not want to fail during the pursuit of the love of his life, so he continued to do nothing in that regard.

Everything about the conference was great. Brock completely enjoyed the daytime meetings—especially the poetry. Experiencing spit from the Christian poets amongst a Christian audience offered a healing intent. The poetic night exceeded all expectations. Each artist represented excellence in his or her calling to speak a poetic word. Witnessing Free Will on the stage was a salty experience for Brock. If he were home alone watching her from his sofa, he would have cried just as the person witnessing a beautiful love story in the cinema. He knew she would be at the conference and enjoyed watching her from afar.

*****

Free Will knows God is in control. She commanded attention as she walked in His will for her life. Kasha, Free Will's girl, has tried everything in her power to block the attention directed to Free Will by Rome. What Kasha does not understand is her competition is not Free Will; her fight is against principalities that block her from seeing her own inner beauty. Nonetheless, Kasha continued to go after the attention of any man who appeared to be interested in Free Will.

From Free Will's perspective, Kasha was doing her a favor by eliminating potential dead wood from her life because any man who was truly interested in her, Kasha will not distract. Rome fell for Kasha's bait months ago. Free Will is respectful to Rome as he comes into her space with his best game, but his pursuit of Free Will is a lost cause.

Free Will's mama always said, "Baby, if anybody takes your man, he was not for you. Move on and let the Lord fight that battle." Free Will believes that if Kasha can steal a man's attention away from her, that man was not designed to handle all she brings to the table. She is not afraid Kasha will hurt her chances of meeting the man who is right for her. This is the season. God placed Kasha in Free Will's circle to weed out weak men. Kasha's season with Free Will is about to end, God has shown Free Will her soul mate.

*****

One week after the International Singles' Conference, Angel officially informed everyone she would pursue a singing career that corresponded with her pursuit for a college degree. Brock also made his decision to attend Howard University School of Medicine. To celebrate their decisions, Brock and his boys went to the Grand Opening of a new coffee café named Jeremiah's Call in their home town where Angel was scheduled to debut as the opening act.

Gratitude for the guilt-free affordable fun, Jeremiah's Call was the place to go for Christians and anyone looking for good clean fun Thursday, Friday and Saturday evenings. The owner offered promotional events to ensure Jeremiah's Call had a balanced mix of male and female customers. The home style menu offered dinner service up to 10:00 p.m.

The theme for Jeremiah's Call was "The truth will set us free." All in the room rested in the freedom to engage in a line dance from time-to-time, hand-dance on occasion and Chicago Steppin' for those who have rehearsed and more. The bottom line rested in the fact that Christians wanted to have good clean fun. They wanted to release endorphins that in turn relieved the toxicants from their spirits brought on by life's struggles.

Brock and his boys really had a good time at the café. The food was exceptional, the comedian funny and Angel brought the house down. Her sultry gospel soul rendition of "Amazing Grace," and her self titled song, "Angel," had the audience standing to their feet. The power of God came down to fill the room. Angel cried as she thanked God and the audience for appreciating her ministry. Brock felt like a very proud big brother. Completely overwhelmed by seeing Angel's ministry on a public stage, Brock said good night to his boys, got up to meet Angel backstage, and looked forward to the ride home with her.

The grand finale was an up and coming artist who had just released a gospel soul/poetry CD. As Brock was leaving with his back to the stage he wondered how anyone could possibly top what had taken place on the stage with Angel's ministry. When Brock was almost out of the door still with his back toward the stage all he could hear was the honey sweet voice of Free Will. The earth stopped—the surreal experience was as mystical as an intense love novel. Brock's heart ached at the thought of moving from under the sweet honey dew of the poetic spit of Free Will. The truth is Brock did not want to miss another chance to get to know his "Dream." Her voice, her sound, her heart, her rhymes rested right on him and it felt good. The decision to not actively pursue Free Will was a past mistake that he was about to rectify.

All who knew her rhymes will not refute the fact that the grace of God flowed through Free Will's pen. Her wet ink, once dried, executed rhymes through her vocal cords that picked up the favor of the Spirit of the living God only to take off from the platform of truth that rested on the biblical teachings in her spirit. She spit truth that landed in the ears of receptive listeners open to catch rhymes that soothed their hurt. Free Will's truth was not afraid that love will not find her. She was not panting, running in place or feverishly looking in strange places for love. The desire to wait on God motivated her in ways that may have some to leap without looking. Waiting with expectancy was her mode of operation. It was in Jeremiah's Call where Free Will stood on the stage that separated her past season from the season standing right in front of her eyes.

The stage was a semi-circle shape surrounded by small round tables that rested a dinner lamp in each center. The dim glow in the room smoothed out facial flaws, and released the feeling of romantic intent. Everyone in the room was free to inhale the atmosphere, with the Christian understanding that recreation does not have to include behaviors that did not please Christ. Enjoyment did include a variety of alcohol-free beverages in celebration of all that was good about flavorful beverages. The beverages offered non-toxic enjoyment as liberation from addictive behavior that sometimes leads to ungodly intent.

Free Will was happiest in front of an audience that grooved to her rhythmic flow without apology, in tune with the Glory of the Lord. Free Will noticed the caring eyes of Brock, which illuminated by the light of the doorway. At the second their eyes met, God changed the direction of her flow. She broke into the song "Sweet Honey Mornin' Dew". The clock stopped. Every person in the room faded into black. They were alone. Every word she spit, broke away every chip, every forgotten birthday, every betrayal from Brock's shoulders. Free Will was speaking to her Dream. Long nights of praying that one day she would see the guy with the deep black eyes again. The eyes that made poetry feel right, that made poetry breathe life into her dead situations. God's grace and mercy covered Free Will as inappropriate suitors tried to work their way into her space. Free Will waited for this day. She saved herself to meet the deep black eyes.

Brock did not move; he could not move. He was stunned by Free Will's ministry, purpose, and free flowing verses. God is good and worthy to be praised for such a time as this. "Please God," Brock prayed for the chance to meet his Dream.

At the end of the set, Free Will asked her assistant to see if Brock would be willing to come backstage for a formal introduction. There was no fear of rejection on her part. Brock turned the corner, approached Free Will, and simply said "Thank you."

CHAPTER EIGHTEEN

Life After the Moment

"… he seats them with princes…"
Psalm 113:8 (NIV)

Angel Johnson:
One Year After the International Singles'
Conference in Atlanta

A NGEL CULTIVATED HER EXTRAORDINARY VOCAL abilities into a gospel-jazz sound that brought people from miles around to fill Jeremiah's Call café on Thursday and Friday evenings. As the singer/song writer/producer, Angel had a local following that threatened to expose her gospel-jazz sound to the nation that was in need of sweet release from the "music as usual vocal experience." Angel's mama, Martha Johnson acted as her manager. Martha was feeling pressure by local demand to hear a CD released from Angel's soulful renditions.

The truth of the matter is, the release of the CD did not frighten Angel, nor did its potential success frighten her; it was the interviewing process. The probing inquiries that could possibly expose the depth of the source in her singing would stop her heart at the thought of revisiting the sexual abuse. Pain associated with the sexual abuse Angel experienced as a young child resulted in a silver lining—diligence to strengthen her vocal cords while singing in the shower. Her vocal cords got stronger as the root of the pain gave color to lyrics.

*****

Angel attends church, sings with the choir, and actively participates in the singles ministry. With a childlike smile, Angel is a great friend to anyone who needs a friend. Although beautiful in appearance, the truth about the lie Angel lives is: Angel is a rape survivor who is afraid to look into the eyes of a man because in a man's eyes she sees the face of her abuser. Having a conversation with a male friend while looking directly in the general direction of his face is not troubling, but looking into his eyes is a major source of pain. In her quest for a breakthrough, Angel continues to seek the face of God. It is in God's presence that Angel finds rest, joy, hope, and optimism for tomorrow. God is the truth and the light that Angel is walking toward to find the grace that will allow her to forgive herself for the wrongs others have committed against her.

*****

A Singles' conference in gorgeous Miami was the place Angel felt beautiful, ready for the world, and prepared to understand her life's purpose. She elected to wake up early for sunrise prayer. The peace of the morning rested in her spirit at the session led by a married couple who led the intercessory prayer team for the conference. Angel felt comfortable under the leadership of a married couple. The couples' union allowed Angel the freedom to pray without judgment from an unmarried peer that may become a potential male suitor. In Angel's mind, single people judge all who come in their space. This is not true when a married couple is in the leadership role.

During the prayer session, once in position to experience God's openness in the intercessory prayer, Angel let go of past fears. It felt good. The Miami Singles' conference was a new beginning for Angel to seek God's answer to her prayers. On the third morning of the prayer session, God clearly showed Angel that it is the Word of God and not the negative comments of her abuser that should shape her opinion of men. Angel regretted imposing the pain of her experience on people who have not done anything to her. Now is the time for Angel to let go, and let God impose His will in her life. This revelation, though difficult to comprehend, is necessary for her to move into her destiny. Angel began to realize that holding on to hurtful memories lent purpose into the hold of the abuser, not allowing the releasing of lyrical expressions. Her way out of oppression was forgiveness. Freed by God's release in prayer, Angel was ready to live.

On the final day of the conference, the intercessory prayer team leaders invited all the intercessors who participated in the Morning Prayer experience as well as those who participated in Late Night Prayer to have dinner that evening at a local five star restaurant. The thought of preparing for a black tie affair was liberating. Angel thought, *What a blessing to have time to fellowship, chit-chat and laugh openly with the many teams of intercessors.* Angel joyfully agreed to attend the festive occasion. Angel purchased a midnight blue cocktail dress that was fitting for the wife of the President of the United States prepared to command the attention at a stately event. She looked stunning with her evening make up and natural hair in a 1960s style afro. It was awesome for Angel to see people from all over the world participating in this eloquent close-out session.

The intercessory leaders had several icebreakers to ease the communication awkwardness. After the social hour, the intercessors ceremoniously strolled through the garden to the dining area experiencing the cool summer breeze on a ninety degree day. A very handsome man walked by Angel. He was strangely familiar, but did not connect to any pictures stacked in Angel's mind. She thought to herself, *Why do I feel like I know this man? I would know if I ever met a man of this stature before.* The gentleman sat next to Angel at dinner and participated in small talk at the table. His full beard, close cut hair, fair complexion and British accent made Angel feel like they had met before, but she could not place him in her experiences. Angel felt joy in her spirit as she thought, *I am attracted to this man. I am not afraid to look directly in his eyes. What is going on with me? Am I delivered from the pain from my abuser?* Angel had a fantastic time at the dinner. She walked to each table to bid farewell to all in the room. She approached the handsome man with the British accent last because she wanted his scent and deep set eyes to stay fresh in her memory. She left the building alone walking one inch off the ground. Angel floated to her hotel thankful that God had permitted her to look into the eyes of a man without feeling hurt.

Angel's hurt remained on the floor of the altar and she, for the first time in her life, was attracted to a man. Angel had to admit the abuser's hurtful comments in the past provided deliverance permissible for her to move on. Angel was comfortable with the fact that she would never see this man again. She continued to think, *Thank you, Jesus, for this feeling. I thank you because I did not think I would ever have this feeling. You are an awesome God worthy of all praise. May your peace rest in my smile so that all who experience it will feel the joy of the Lord?* On the way to the hotel, Angel felt like skipping. It just never once occurred to Angel that the attention was mutual.

Wanting to savor the experience, Angel took her time walking back to the hotel. Her more moderately priced hotel was four blocks away from the restaurant. The hotel had a gorgeous fountain in the front. She sat on the fountain edge to reflect and toss coins into its base. Angel completely forgot to turn on her cell phone before she left the restaurant. Unbeknownst to Angel, her roommates were trying to reach her for over an hour. They were worried out of their minds. When she opened the door to the room, Angel heard Nancy and Kasha say, "Angel, where have you been? We have been trying to reach you for over an hour. Why is your cell phone off?" Completely overwhelmed by the bombardment of questions, Angel just stood there and shrugged her shoulders. "Well, anyway," Nancy said, "Prince Alexander Buckington requests your company for breakfast 9:00 a.m. tomorrow morning at the same hotel in which you had dinner tonight." Very perplexed, Angel said to Nancy, "I do not know a Prince Alexander Buckington." Nancy said, "He said to tell you he is Aubrey, the man you sat next to at dinner tonight." Nancy and Kasha had given their life to Christ. They attended the conference as guest of Angel's who has agreed to support them in their new Christian walk.

After many years of carrying the evil words of her abuser, God lifted the hurt in a moment. The joy of feeling peace in the presence of a man bubbled up in her spirit as she said, "I would love to go. Who do I need to call to accept the invitation?" "He is on the phone right now." Nancy and Kasha said in unison, "He would not hang up until you came in." Nancy went on to say, "Take the phone Angel and speak to this man—Please." Nancy put the phone to her ear and Angel said, "Yes, Aubrey, I would love to meet you for breakfast."

Prologue

A NGEL DID NOT RECOGNIZE ALEX, Free Will's cousin, until he reintroduced himself at breakfast. Aubrey, who she originally was introduced to as Alex back in high school, watched her from afar over the years, told Angel how his Nigerian mother told him the story of the Great Nigerian business man who traveled to America to see if he could make it in America. The executive made it to America, married an American, and had two children, a boy, and a girl. The business man went back home to visit his family and was lost at sea. He was so in love with his wife and children that his spirit appeared as an angel who protected his family.

Angel looked over at the next table and winked at Poppa as he watched the conversation with the approval of a Nigerian business man. When Alex glanced to see what had captured Angel's attention, no one was there. Poppa could finally rest in peace because Angel had found her prince.

CHAPTER NINETEEN

Poetic Expressions
Of a New Order

Deuteronomy 17:8 (KJV)

"If there arise a matter too hard for thee in judgment, between blood and blood, between plea and plea, and between stroke and stroke, being matters of controversy within thy gates: then shalt thou arise, and get thee up into the place which the LORD thy God shall choose."

Who Matters

It is the chatter about me
Chatter you participate in
I thought you were my girl
I thought you were my friend

In your eyes we both see
We both know it is true
Hypocrite comes to mind
The Bah-Bah-Bah your speech makes me blue

Enemy acting as a friend
Do not join in the chatter spin
Stay focused on what God has for you
I will be waiting at the finish line when God sees us through

Chatter of the negative spin
May defer the Destiny of friends
God's unconditional love will see us through
A real desire to stay your friend—a friend who is true
to you

As angry as you make me
You bring out the best in me
Your negative chatter brought me to my knees
I learned peace, patience, and tolerance from God
The only one who matters to me.

Isaiah 30:9 (KJV)

"That this is a rebellious people, lying children, children that will not hear the law of the LORD."

A Grandma's Plea to her Daughter

Because you're hurt,
You have increased the possibility of your daughter having a major life void

Because you're hurt,
You are pushing your daughter to want to know her daddy more

Because you're hurt,
You are contributing to the population of women who are searching for the eyes of a man they want to adore

Because you're hurt,
Your little girl may grow up to do whatever it takes to get a man, to love a man, to kiss a man and more

Why can't you see that your daughter will see her daddy's flaws?

Why can't you see that she will see what you see, know and still love him "just because?"

Why can't you see that hurt people and you are contributing to a nation of damaged little girls?

Why can't you see that keeping your daughter from the first man in her life is helping to make him into a super hero?

No one is perfect, not even you,
Do not be the judge and jury by not allowing your daughter to meet the first man in her life even though he has moved on from you.

Joyfully participate in her pursuit of her happiness remedy with visions of warm daddy's little girl hugs with her head resting in his chest.

Let your daughter meet her daddy; trust God to do the rest.

Be a gallant woman of God.

Do the right thing, and you will be blessed.

2 Samuel 7:28 (KJV)

"And now, O Lord GOD, thou art that God, and thy words be true, and thou hast promised this goodness unto thy servant."

Tears Drop

Tears of the promise DROP

From our EYES

Fall into the PRAYERS

Of our DREAMS

Later evaporating into the CLOUDS

That later RAINS

Onto PROMISES

For our ASPIRATIONS

That's when the promise of GOD

DROPS

Onto the HOPE

To EVOLVE

Into the PATH

Of God's DESTINY

For our LIFE

Philippians 3:8 (KJV)

*"Yea doubtless, and I count all things but loss for the excellency of
the knowledge of Christ Jesus my Lord: for whom I have suffered
the loss of all things, and do count them but dung, that
I may win Christ."*

Breakthrough

Hearing my voice out loud

Beautiful

Cynical

Pronounced—Lovely

Alone with Song

Perfecting

New

Timed—Magical

Safe in the only way a song will rise

Not abused

Run down

Overwhelmed—Survived

Surprise them with all I do

Wait

Daddy's coming

Mommy's here to appreciate the tune.

2 Thessalonians 3:5 (KJV)

And the Lord direct your hearts into the love of God, and into the patient waiting for Christ.

The Flower Dance

The petals fall

    He loves me

        He loves me not

At a distant, I wait and watch

    Pray my heart's Dream notices me

        Pray my Dream has a two-sided theme

Watch me wonder

    Wonder whether the experience will feel like

    Heaven

        Wonder if the experience will feel like hell

        Only God knows for sure what is in my

        Dream's head

    Will this letter reach his ears?

        Will this letter penetrate his heart like a

        spear?

The petals fall

    He loves me

        He loves me not

One more petal to go

    God knows the answer

        Is it "yes" or is it "no"?

Psalm 145:7 (KJV)

"They shall abundantly utter the memory of thy great goodness, and shall sing of thy righteousness."

Memory

Through the cornea splats the glimpse of an uncomfortable
memory

Why did he, I mean she, or should I say they, do that?

It felt strange, bad, made me mad

Actions, words, and deeds that identify me as the less than special

No one spoke up for me

I know they heard my plight

They looked into my eyes and saw empty space

In the house, everybody knew I was home alone with the abuser

Everyone knew it was not right

They looked the other way

They saw my shame and later anger in my eyes

The eyes that would not allow me to look straight into the eyes of
Love

Until I released the pain into Praise

Praise, Prayer and Purpose took my pain to the altar

When I got up from my knees, Pain stayed

God took the Pain away

The Memory remains to help others not falter.

CHAPTER TWENTY

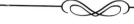

Songs of Freedom

"…He entered a house and did not want anyone to know it; yet he could not keep his presence secret."
Mark 7:24 (NIV)

Do you have secret(s) that motivate you to seek healing or destruction? Give examples.

_____

_____

_____

_____

_____

_____

_____

_____

_____

The Truth About the Lie I Live

"But speaking the truth in love, may grow up into him in all things, which is the head, even Christ:*"*
(Ephesians 4:13-15 KJV)

Everybody has something about himself or herself that he or she is not ready to share with the world. Is the information you are not sharing holding you back or helping you to succeed?

_____

_____

_____

_____

_____

_____

_____

_____

_____

_____

A New Life Order

*When I say to a wicked man, 'You will surely die,' and you do not
warn him or speak out to dissuade him from his evil ways in order to save his
life, that wicked man will die for his sin, and I will hold you accountable
for his blood.*
Ezekiel 3:18 (NIV)

Have you ever witnessed someone with sinful behavior, had an
opportunity to speak to him or her about the goodness of the Lord,
and did not? If you accepted the assignment and had the conversation,
what happened?

_____

_____

_____

_____

_____

_____

_____

_____

The Last Shall Be First

"But many that are first shall be last; and the last shall be first."
Matthew 19:30 *(KJV)*

Does being first at one stage in your life mean you will be first forever?
Reflect on how it feels or not feel to move from last to first?

_____

_____

_____

_____

_____

_____

_____

_____

_____

_____

Freedom

"I will walk about in freedom, for I have sought out your precepts."
Psalm 119:45 (NIV)

What does it feel like to walk in the Will of God? What does it feel like to ignore the Will of God?

_____

_____

_____

_____

_____

_____

_____

_____

_____

_____

The Oil and Water Mix

"Then I will let her waters settle and make her streams flow like oil, declares the Sovereign LORD."
Ezekiel 32:14 (NIV)

Do you know someone that can see and speak to your indiscretions (e.g. lying, cheating, stealing, addictions and more) that other people over look? How do you feel about that person? Are you happy when you see him or her coming? If not, why?

_____

_____

_____

_____

_____

_____

_____

_____

_____

Best Friends

"A man of many companions may come to ruin, but there is a friend who sticks closer than a brother."
Proverbs 18:24 (NIV)

Do you classify people as best friend, friend, or associate? If so, why is it important to classify people? What standards are used to classify a person as a friend?

_____

_____

_____

_____

_____

_____

_____

_____

_____

Enemy Intent

The enemy boasted, 'I will pursue, I will overtake them. I will divide the spoils; I will gorge myself on them. I will draw my sword and my hand will destroy them.'
Exodus 15:9 (NIV)

Do you ever fraternize with the enemy? Does the enemy know you know their intent?

_____

_____

_____

_____

_____

_____

_____

_____

_____

The Next Level

"Your beginnings will seem humble, so prosperous will your future be."
Job 8:7 (NIV)

Do you have long term goals? If so, what are your goals? If not, why? How does having goals help change questionable behavior?

_____

_____

_____

_____

_____

_____

_____

_____

_____

College Days

"The Teacher searched to find just the right words, and what he wrote was upright and true."
Ecclesiastes 12:10 (NIV)

How do you communicate without offending someone when you offer friendly advice regarding what you think and feel about life's issues?

Follow Your Heart

"Obey them not only to win their favor when their eye is on you, but like slaves of Christ, doing the will of God from your heart."
Ephesians 6:6 (NIV)

Can you articulate your heart's desire? If yes, are you following it? If not, why?

_____

_____

_____

_____

_____

_____

_____

_____

_____

_____

An Answered Prayer

"So we fasted and petitioned our God about this, and he answered our prayer."
Ezra 8:23 (NIV)

Do you know what it feels like to have an answered prayer? If not, can you imagine what an answered prayer would feel like? Describe.

_____

_____

_____

_____

_____

_____

_____

_____

_____

_____

After the Letter

This is what the LORD says: "In the time of my favor I will answer you, and in the day of salvation I will help you; I will keep you and will make you to be a covenant for the people, to restore the land and to reassign its desolate inheritances."
Isaiah 49:8 (NIV)

When something good and exciting happens to you, do you feel happy or do you prepare for something bad to happen?

_____

_____

_____

_____

_____

_____

_____

_____

_____

The Rice in Your Puddin'

"When wisdom entereth into thine heart, and knowledge is pleasant unto thy soul; Discretion shall preserve thee, understanding shall keep thee."
Proverbs 2:10-11 (KJV)

Who has come into your life to help you become a better person? Describe your relationship. If not, how do you feel about that?

_____

_____

_____

_____

_____

_____

_____

_____

The Evil Behind the Smile

"The face of the LORD is against those who do evil, to cut off the memory of them from the earth."
Psalm 34:16 (NIV)

Has anyone that treated you inappropriately ever taken the time to apologize to you? Describe. If not, would you accept their apology now?

_____

_____

_____

_____

_____

_____

_____

_____

_____

The Apology

*"To give his people the knowledge of salvation through the forgiveness
of their sins."*
Luke 1:77 (NIV)

Will a letter of apology suffice for the hurt and abuse you experienced
in the past? If not, what would be an acceptable remedy?

_____

_____

_____

_____

_____

_____

_____

_____

_____

Thank You Opens the Door to...
You're Welcome

"As you enter the home, give it your greeting."
Matthew 10:12 (NIV)

_____

_____

_____

_____

_____

_____

_____

_____

_____

_____

_____

_____

Life After the Moment

" ... he seats them with princes..."
Psalm 113:8 NIV

Are you able to trust God to walk you through your destination or are you in the driver's seat? If you are driving, why is it hard to trust God?

_____

_____

_____

_____

_____

_____

_____

_____

_____

_____

_____

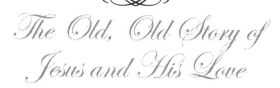

The Old, Old Story of Jesus and His Love

YOU HAVE JUST FINISHED READING *The Truth About the Lie I Live*. Allow me to share with you the old, old story of the Gospel of the Lord Jesus Christ. If you are not already a Christian, here is how you can know the Lord for yourself:

1. **Accept the fact that you are a sinner, and that you have broken God's law.** The Bible says in Ecclesiastes 7:20: *"For there is not a just man upon earth that doeth good, and sinneth not."* Romans 3:23: *"For all have sinned and come short of the glory of God."*

2. **Accept the fact that there is a penalty for sin.** The Bible states in Romans 6:23: *"For the wages of sin is death..."*

3. **Accept the fact that you are on the road to hell.** Jesus Christ said in Matthew 10:28: *"And fear not them which kill the body, but are not able to kill the soul: but rather fear him which is able to destroy both soul and body in hell."*

The Bible says in Revelation 21:8: *"But the fearful, and unbelieving, and the abominable, and murderers, and whoremongers and sorcerers, and idolaters, and all liars, shall have their part in the lake which burneth with fire and brimstone: which is the second death."*

4. Accept the fact that you cannot do anything to save yourself! The Bible states in Ephesians 2: 8, 9: *"For by grace are ye saved through faith: and that not of yourselves: it is a gift of God. Not of works, lest any man should boast."*

5. Accept the fact that God loves you more than you love yourself, and that He wants to save you from hell. *"For God so loved the world, that He gave His only begotten Son, that whosoever believeth in Him should not perish, but have everlasting life."* (John 3:16)

6. With these facts in mind, please repent of your sins, believe on the Lord Jesus Christ and pray and ask Him to come into your heart and save you this very moment.

The Bible states in the book of Romans 10:9, 13: *"That if thou shalt confess with thy mouth the Lord Jesus, and shalt believe in thine heart that God hath raised Him from the dead, thou shalt be saved." "For whosoever shall call upon the name of the Lord shall be saved."*

7. If you are willing to trust Christ as your Saviour, please pray with me the following prayer:

> Heavenly Father, I realize that I am a sinner. For Jesus Christ's sake, please forgive me of my sins. I now believe with all of my heart that Jesus Christ died, was buried, and rose again. Lord Jesus, please come into my heart and save my soul and change my life. Amen.

About the Author

C. NATASHA RICHBURG HAS BEEN married to her husband, Melvin, for over 27 years. She is the mother of four children. Mrs. Richburg is a preacher, teacher, and speaker positioned to bring forth illustrations in her short stories that draw us to find reflection that offer recipes of contemplative solutions. She believes we are a village of people who have experiences to share—experiences as presented to the reader through the characters in her books.

Mrs. Richburg has a Masters of Business Administration from Morgan State University and a Masters in Information Systems from Johns Hopkins University. She has attended, and completed many courses at St. Mary's Seminary in Baltimore. Mrs. Richburg is currently attending Morgan State University in pursuit of a Doctorate in Urban Leadership Education. Mrs. Richburg professes Proverbs 24:5 (KJV) which says: ***"[a] wise man is strong; yea a man of knowledge increaseth strength."***

5402002R0

Made in the USA
Charleston, SC
10 June 2010